MINSTEAD

MINSTEAD

Life in a 17th Century New Forest Community

by

PETER ROBERTS

To Stan & Bill

Best Wishes

Peter.

NOVA FORESTA PUBLISHING

First published 2002 by
Nova Foresta Publishing
185 Lyndhurst Road, Ashurst, Southampton, SO40 7AR

Printed by BAS Printers Limited
Over Wallop, Hampshire

ISBN 0 9523173 3 8

Contents

Appendices

Illustrations

Acknowledgements

I have received assistance from a variety of organisations and individuals and would like to thank all those who have helped me in my quest for knowledge whether or not they are mentioned below.

This work started life as a dissertation at Portsmouth University, it failed to appear at the correct time and whilst I no longer live in hope of high marks from my former tutors I would like to record my thanks to them. It proved to be a fascinating year with the enthusiasm and criticism of James Thomas at the forefront. John Chapman also provided valuable criticism at a vital stage: 'where is this going?' set me thinking afresh.

The staff at Hampshire Record Office have maintained their unfailing courtesy and helpfulness and deserve particular thanks. Similarly assistance has been sought and received at West Sussex Record Office and the Public Record Office. Libraries at various locations throughout Hampshire including the University of Southampton have been of great value. The library of the New Forest 9th Centenary Trust at Lyndhurst has proved to be an extremely useful local asset. It has often provided me with a quick and easily obtainable answer, my thanks to the staff there.

Amongst individuals who have been particularly helpful in various ways, providing background information, sharing the fruits of their research, and debating some points, have been David Stagg and Richard Reeves. Some like Peter Jameson have provided great assistance on specific subjects and often led me to others such as Laurie Gardner who have in their turn helped me. Ronda Purkess is amongst a number of people who might describe themselves as family historians but actually know as much about a locality as many local historians. Similar help has been received from Martin Biggs, Bill Perry, Eunice Price, Bill Marsh and Tessa Davis.

A number of the villagers in Minstead have provided me with a great deal of information. They have loaned material, allowed me to peruse their deeds, look at their property and share some of their knowledge of the area built up over a lifetime. To Peter Green, Tim Selwood, Dennis Hickman, Nick and Jeannie Mellersh, Malcolm and Janet McCarraher, Heidi Bone, Andrew Trend, Howard Wilkinson, Irene Corrigan, Noelle Chambers, Stan Gibbons, Annie Cooper and the villagers of Minstead, many thanks.

Others who have provided assistance, but do not fit easily into categories, are Eric Byford of Forest Row, Barry Peckham, Rosemary Manning, Jimmy Winter, Arthur Lloyd, Jude James, Georgina Babey, The Cambridge Preservation Society, Compton Estate Office at Castle Ashby, Northampton Library. If I have omitted anybody, please take this as a thank you. It goes without saying that any mistakes or errors that remain are mine and mine alone.

Preface

There has been little detailed work on the Forest economy in the century prior to 1700. Tubbs in his admirable overview, first published in 1986, offers some background but little detail of this period. This is an attempt to fill that gap by providing evidence of the lives of the people of a village that was (and is) intimately linked with the Forest and of their reliance upon it for their subsistence.

Although few exactly contemporary sources exist for the study of Minstead in the 17th century there are sufficient at a reasonably close date for an outline of life in the middle of the century to be examined. Taking the period 1650-70 as a base, but realising that there would be change in that period, it is possible to establish some concept of who lived in the village and an idea of how they spent their days. A written survey of the lands of Richard Compton together with records of the courts held between 1652 and 1656 provide not only a major source but evidence of the continuance of a manorial system that was decaying even as it was being written. The later court rolls provide, at best, a description of land changing hands and, at worst, no more than a record of who appeared on the court day. Similarly churchwardens accounts have not survived before 1641 and there are large gaps later in the century.

Most descriptions of Forest people have relied upon surviving forest court records and tax returns which, although useful, allow little detail of their lives to permeate through. The houses of the inhabitants usually provide copious information as to the lives of their occupiers. Unfortunately only a few of the more substantial buildings of the well to do yeoman farmers have survived. Cob hovels which received a mention in a report of 1787, and may have been in existence in the 17th century, are no longer extant. Writers and travellers from around 1800 have left descriptions of the lives of the local populace. They often interpreted what they saw without sufficient investigation or appreciation of the local resources. This is an attempt to give voice to those villagers by using their own words and those of their contemporaries through their wills and inventories.

I have not limited my work to studying these sources but have supplemented it with other local material, much of it found in the manorial court records and the government tax returns referred to above. To put it into perspective I have consulted the works of some contemporary writers and modern authorities for a wider interpretation where appropriate.

The area covered by the work is in the main the present district known as Minstead and London Minstead together with that part of Emery Down falling within the manor boundary. The outlying areas of Stoney Cross, Acres Down and part of Newtown do not appear to have been settled until the 18th and 19th centuries. Their history is almost certainly linked with the emparking that occurred when the Comptons sold their Bisterne estate and moved to Minstead at the end of the 18th century. Although Canterton with part of Cadnam was within the parish and Bartley was linked with London Minstead for administrative reasons, these settlements are not central to this study but are referred to where relevant.

To set the work in context the opening chapter deals with the background of the major landowning family, the Comptons. This is followed by a study of the Forest and its administration as it is (imprecisely) understood today. Much new research has been undertaken on this by the author and others (notably Richard Reeves) in recent years. The book then describes the manorial system in Minstead and proceeds to work through various aspects of life of the people, their farming methods, animals and crops. Further chapters cover the food they ate and the homes they lived in. Few were full time farmers, nearly all had a second occupation usually linked to use of local materials. Minstead was the centre of Hampshire's charcoal making industry for several centuries. A section follows on the social consequences of their lives, the wealth and poverty, the disputes, the law and the church, and the change that was wreaked upon lives by national events.

Units and Editorial notes

The units that have been used throughout are those that were in use at the time. Therefore pounds, shillings, and pence are mainly used. Twelve pence made one shilling, equivalent to five modern pence and so twenty shillings to the pound. Forty perch were one rood and four roods made an acre. Two and a half acres are equal to a hectare. Spellings are usually quoted as found which, if not obvious, a more usual form may be supplied in square brackets. This may look odd to the modern eye and will occasionally result in varied renderings of a name such as Osmand or Osmond within one paragraph but is retained for the sake of authenticity. Who is to say which was 'correct' three hundred years ago? Square brackets [ ] are used throughout to indicate omissions or comments.

DEDICATED TO THE COMMONERS OF MINSTEAD,

PAST, PRESENT AND FUTURE

1 Setting and the Sinews of Power

From the moment that I turned up out of Lyndhurst, I seemed to have entered an ancient region... Open knolls, and ascending woodlands on one side, covered with majestic beeches, and the village children playing under them; on the other, the most rustic cottages, almost buried in the midst of their orchard trees, and thatched... The beehives in their rustic rows; the little crofts, all belong to a primitive country... As I advanced, heathery hills stretched away on one hand; woods came down thickly and closely on the other, and a winding road beneath the shade of large old trees, conducted me to one of the most retired and peaceful of hamlets. It was Minstead.[1]

William Howitt's description though written in the mid 19th century could still apply to the Minstead of the Stuart era; little change appears to have taken place in the way of life, the cottages may have been replaced, but the Lord of the Manor was still a Compton and sustenance was provided directly by working the land and grazing animals on the commons and the New Forest. Even the Inn, *The Trusty Servant*, though much added to, remained the same alongside the village green just down the hill from the church.[2]

SITUATION

Minstead is virtually surrounded by forest, only on the southern tip where it adjoins Lyndhurst is it bordered by cultivated land. The parish contained 10,382 acres, much of this termed extraparochial where it formed part of the New Forest. The enclosed lands in the mid 17th century encompassed an area of perhaps 450-500 acres.[3] It was surrounded by the unenclosed waste lands of the manor which in turn were encircled by 92,000 acres of the New Forest and adjacent commons, much of it commonable. The Manor of Minstead formed the nucleus of the village, it resembles a tilted egg with its base resting on the slopes of Northerwood and its apex at Stoney Cross. Minor changes to this basic shape occurred in the 19th century and major transformations took place in the 20th with two large land sales after the wars.

GEOLOGY and DRAINAGE

Much of the northern part of Minstead is situated on a band of Barton Clay that stretches westwards across the Forest from Dibden. It is capped on the higher ground at Stoney Cross and Malwood by Plateau Gravel. Barton Sand shows through close to the Gravel and forms the basis of the southern lands from a line south of the Church to the Kennels and extending on through most of Emery Down to Lyndhurst.

The land is drained in a general north-west to south-east direction by three streams, Dogben Gutter, the Fleet and the Mill Stream, all feed the Bartley Water, eventually emptying into the sea by Eling Tide Mill. The source of all three is close to the Gravel Plateau, each have to wind around numerous small hills. Little of the land is completely flat, that around The Park and Football Green in the east being the least inclined.

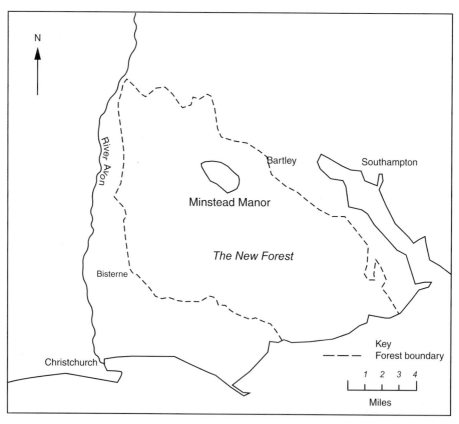

Fig 1 **Position of Minstead Manor within the New Forest**

ORIGINS

The Manors of Bisterne and Minstead together with land at Crow near Ringwood and Totton have been linked at least since the time of the Conqueror when they were held by the sons of Godric Malf.[4] It is likely that the name of Malf provides the origin of Malwood to the north of Minstead village. These lands passed through the Berkeley family and into the hands of Werburgh Brewerton before her second marriage, to William Compton brought them into the Compton family around 1513/4.[5]

William Compton was a friend of the Duke of York, later Henry VIII, who rewarded him richly for services provided in the field of battle; he received a knighthood following the French campaign of 1513 at a time when he was sheriff of Hampshire. Evidently a favourite of the King, he held many other appointments and gained a fortune in the process for when he died he retained land in eighteen counties. Cardinal Wolsley was the first guardian to William Compton's son Peter (1523-1544).[6] His second guardian was the Earl of Shrewsbury, who became his father-in-law upon Peter Compton's marriage to daughter Anne. Although Peter Compton died aged only 21 he left a son, Henry (1544-1589), who was created Lord Compton of Compton in 1572. This Compton was one of the peers who tried Mary, Queen of Scots. Henry Compton's first son, William, became the first Earl of Northampton, thereby inheriting the major part of his fathers' estates.[7]

SIR HENRY COMPTON

Sir Henry Compton was the third son, though the first born of his father's second marriage to Anne, daughter of Sir John Spencer of Allthorp, Northants. He inherited (amongst others) the Hampshire estates including the Manors of Bisterne and Minstead.[8] Educated at Christ Church College, Oxford, matriculating in June 1599 aged 15 he proceeded to Lincoln's Inn in 1602. There he received a training in the law and became an associate of the bench two years later.[9] He married the 2nd Earl of Dorset's daughter, Cicely Sackville, in the early years of the century; they had two or three sons and three daughters. Their marriage was not always easy as Lady Anne Clifford writing in 1619 noted that '...they were about to separate, when she was to have a hundred a year and the child...'[10] A permanent separation did not occur as Cicely's sister-in-law later helped bring about a reconciliation.[11] The marital difficulties appeared to follow their removal from London around 1616 to Brambletye, Sussex living in what has been described as a 'damp moated house.'[12] Any difficulties that remained

Fig 2 **Ruins of Brambletye House**

were overcome by her death which occurred within five years.[13] Brambletye House (now a ruin) was built by Sir Henry Compton for his second wife Mary, daughter of Sir George Browne, second son of Viscount Montague of Bourton. Over the doorway of this house may still be seen the Compton's coat of arms impaled with that of the Browne's. Much higher is the date 1631 and the initials H.M.C.[14]

The Compton connection with the Sackville family had started through Sir Henry's mother's third marriage to Robert Sackville in 1592, Sir Henry continuing it by becoming a trustee for Sackville College at East Grinstead, Sussex in the 1630's and early 1640's.[15] He became MP for East Grinstead in 1601, a seat he held for much of the next forty years, and which was almost certainly secured through his connection with the Sackvilles. His youngest daughter, Margaret took the connection through to a third generation by her second marriage to Colonel Thomas Sackville.[16] Sir Henry Compton lived much of his adult life, at Brambletye House, Sussex, though he had a London address in Finch Lane in the heart of the capital and appears to have used stewards to run his many estates in several counties.[17] His interests extended to industry as well as land for he was a director of a Westminster Company of Soapmakers.[18]

Fig 3 **Sir Henry Compton from a painting at Compton Wynyates**

At James I's Coronation in 1603 he was created a Knight of the Bath, and appointed Custos Brevium 'keeper of the briefs' in the Court of Common Pleas in December the following year. An office worth £2,000 per annum, and supposedly granted for life.[19] He was, however, relieved of the post after 1636 when he was required to enter into an £8,000 bond.[20] He was active at both local and national levels, his work as a Justice of the Peace being recorded at East Grinstead Assizes from 1624, and that as a Ranger of Ashdown Forest from 1630.[21] The latter appointment though, would have been a sinecure. He was made a Deputy Lieutenant of Sussex in 1624, a position which ultimately brought him into conflict with other MP's because of his loyalty to the King.[22] His support for the Royalist cause was such that he was committed to the Tower of London in 1643. Following his release, upon bail, he was required to stay within 10 miles of London excepting the counties of Sussex, Surrey, Hampshire and Kent.[23]

The distrust of Parliament towards Sir Henry Compton and his family was increased by the knowledge that his second wife, Mary, was a papist. Much of his property in several counties including estates in Hampshire, Northamptonshire, Essex, Norfolk, Somerset, Lancashire and Yorkshire was the subject of Sequestration orders by the Committee for Compounding. The County Committee for Norfolk observed of his widow, Mary in 1650:

> ...but we hold it impossible for her ladyship to produce any authentic certificate of her non-conviction for recusancy, in regard of the several assizes, sessions, counties, and cities, at which she may have been convicted, the clerks of whom may have records of the fact.

> It is clear that Parliament adjudged Papists and popishly affected prelates as the first formentors of our intestine war, and therefore as the most equitable objects of sequestration, and ordained two-thirds of every Papist,

without any limitation or qualification, to be sequestrated; and unless that
ordinance is repealed, there is no colour of excuse for any Papist, though
not convicted, from sequestration. Lady Compton is vulgarly known to
have been a professed ancient Popish recusant, and we know her to be not
only within the ordinance of 19 Aug. 1643, but also the former one of 31
March 1643; had she then been a widow, she might easily then, as now,
have been convicted by witnesses of recusancy; but being notably known
to be a Papist, the late committee, after her husband's death, and before
Michaelmas last, sequestrated $^2/_3$ of her estate; and she neglecting for 2
or 3 months to offer any excuse, either by taking the oath of abjuration
or otherwise, the half year's rent due last Michaelmas was collected to
the use of the State; but all sequestrations being suspended for a while by
the late Act of Parliament, we, according to our power and instructions,
re-sequestrated her estate.[24]

Sir Henry Compton's previous wealth and difficulties with the Parliamentarians
is shown by the assessment that was made and requested of him in 1643 by the
Committee for the Advance of Money, which was for £1,200. In May 1645 he
was brought into custody for non-payment and the following July when reas-
sessed at £3,000, evidence was produced that he held £2,000 belonging to Mrs
Arundel, a papist.[25] At the time of his death in Paris in December 1648 Sir
Henry, having been declared a delinquent for bearing arms against Parliament,
was still negotiating terms with the various Committees for Compounding.[26]

RICHARD COMPTON

Henry's eldest son Richard had no property of his own until he inherited many
of his fathers estates and recovered them by compounding.[27] He appears to have
concentrated on the Hampshire properties; certainly he sold two Manors in
Gloucestershire in 1651, probably to pay his fines.[28] Richard was born in 1604
and like many heirs to large estates received an education in law, being admitted
to Gray's Inn in 1634.[29] Although he did not inherit his father's property until
1650 he was evidently living locally before that as he is listed as one of the 'free
burgesses' of Lymington in 1649.[30] The Court Baron held in April 1652 for the
Manor of Minstead and Brook contains a full list of the cottagers, freeholders,
copyholders and widows together with a note of the customs of the Manor. It is
the first surviving record of the Manor under Richard Compton and appears by
its detail to be the first held by him as Lord of the Manor.[31] It is not until 1655
that a survey, by Jonathan Godfrey, of his estates in Hampshire shows him to
possess Manors at Bisterne, Totton and Bartley, Exbury and Lepe as well as
other tenements and farms in and around the New Forest.[32] He married Amey

Warre, daughter of Henry Warre of Horton, Illminster, Somerset in 1656. They had three children, Richard, baptised February 1657/8, who did not survive infancy, Amey, baptised June 1660, and Henry, baptised four years later who eventually succeeded his father.[33] Richard and Amey lived at Bisterne Manor, a large house, still standing, set in its own orchards and gardens extending to nearly five acres.[34] He made additions to it, probably in 1652 (the date over the door alongside the Compton Coat-of-Arms), and remained there for over thirty years until his death in July 1684 aged 80.[35]

Fig 4 **Bisterne Manor House, probably of Elizabethan origin**

Several of Richard Compton's kinsfolk showed great spirit; his step brother Henry supported the Earl of Holland against parliament and later, in 1649, was required to leave England and 'not return without leave.'[36]
However he returned within a year for he was imprisoned in the Tower of London for accepting a challenge from Thomas Howard the son of Lord Howard but released on condition that he would not further the dispute. He could not resist a challenge though for within eighteen months he had been killed in a duel with Lord Chandos.[37] Cecilia Compton, Richard's eldest sister, who had married Henry, heir to the 2nd Lord Arundell had defended Wardour Castle from the Parliamentarians with her mother-in-law for nine days during 1643 before being forced to surrender.[38] George, another step brother to Richard Compton, was also in the King's Army and forced to compound but appears to have gone mad and had the judgement made against him respited.[39] As a Royalist Richard Compton was subject to the 'decimation tax' of 1655 following the uprising of that year. Whether he posed a real or imaginary threat is uncertain, what is known is that he was assessed to pay the sixth highest amount in Hampshire.[40] In any event, whether less spirited or more pragmatic than some of his kin, he decided to renounce his former ways and took the oath of abjuration in 1657.[41] Although he held no high office of state, Richard Compton took an interest in local affairs following the restoration, captaining a troop of volunteers in the Hampshire Militia from 1660, managing his estates and becoming a JP in 1669.[42] Following his death in 1684, and burial at Ringwood, the estates passed to his surviving son Henry.[43]

Both Sir Henry Compton and Richard Compton took care to maintain the value of their rights in the New Forest. The often quoted claim Richard Compton made at the Justice Seat of 1670 in which he claims the right of vicinage for the Manor on account of his waste lands adjoining those of the forest but within the bounds of the New Forest, is in fact merely a repeat of an assertion made by his father, Sir Henry Compton in 1635.[44] Percival Lewis, writing in 1811, regarded the claim made by Richard Compton as 'particularly moderate'; it has however served the successive Lords of the Manor and their tenants well.[45] It has enabled them to maintain their stock on the forest without paying any dues for this privilege 'from a time before the memory of man'.[46] The only loss they have had is that of rights pertaining to turbary and marl; rights which they had within the Manor in any case.

Fig 5 **19th century copy of 1635 forest claim of Sir H Compton**

Proscribed from high office because of his (suspected) beliefs and therefore ineligible for forest appointments Richard Compton was nevertheless required to attend the Swainmote Courts at Lyndhurst as a freeholder from 1661 to 1669.[47] His father, Sir Henry, had attended the justice seat held at Lyndhurst and presided over by Henry earl of Holland in September 1634 but failed to appear at Swainmote Courts and was fined.[48]

Notes

1   William Howitt, *The Rural Life of England*, 1838, 3rd ed 1862 pp. 368-9
2   HRO 11M59/E2/286240, Deeds of *The Trusty Servant*, 16th December 1837. The Inn was the subject of a thousand year lease in 1602
3   458 acres are made up by the 1655 survey figure of 247 acres together with a further 211 acres shown in the 1670 New Forest claims. In addition an allowance must be made for encroachers not then claiming and any new manorial enclosures between 1655-1670
4   Julian Munby, Ed *Domesday Book, Hampshire* 1982, Chichester, entry numbers 69,39; NF9,37; NF9,38; NF9,39

5 W. B. Compton, *History of the Comptons of Compton Wynyates*, 1930, p. 73. Werburg Brewerton 1488-1525 was previously married to Sir Francis Cheyney. The exact date she married Sir William Compton has not been ascertained. George Matcham's Hundred of Frustfield in Sir Richard Colt Hoare's *History of Modern Wiltshire*, 1844 p. 49 indicates this date. The heir, Peter, was born in 1523

6 *Dictionary of National Biography*, 1887 Vol xi p. 453

7 Rupert Kepple, *History of the Compton Family*, 1928, p. 10

8 P W Hasler, The History of Parliament HMSO 1981, *The House of Commons 1558-1603*, Vol 1 p. 636

9 Joseph Foster, *Alumni Oxonienses 1500-1714* Vol 1, p. 314

10 George C Williamson, *Lady Anne Clifford Countess of Dorset, Pembroke and Montgomery, 1590-1676: Her life, letters and work,* 1967 reprint, Wakefield, p. 111

11 Ibid, p. 129. Anne Clifford was Sir Henry Compton's sister-in-law

12 Eric Byford, *Aspects of the History of Brambletye,* pp. 9-24 in Forest Row Vol 4, No 3, Feb 1990. A visit by the author in January 1999 confirmed the description of the site

13 J S Cockburn, Ed, *Calendar of Assize Records, Sussex Indictments, James I*, 1975 HMSO, p. 143

14 They would appear to have been living in the old moated house for four of their six children are noted in the local Church registers between 1625-1630. Sussex Record Society Vol XXIV *Register of East Grinstead 1558-1661* pp. 90, 91, 96 and 175

15 P W Hasler, op. cit., p. 636. WSRO Add. Ms. 17,842 Accounts of Sackville College, East Grinstead 1637-1642

16 Rupert Kepple, op. cit., p. 16

17 Thomas Walker Horsfield F.S.A., *History of Sussex*, Volume 1, 1835, p. 388. George C Williamson, op. cit., p. 129

18 *Calendar of State Papers Domestic, 1637-8,* p. 299; *CSP Dom.* 18 July 1640, p. 491

19 *CSP Dom. 1603-10*, p. 173

20 *CSP Dom. 1636-37*, p. 268

21 J S Cockburn, op. cit., pp. 134, 143, 144

22 *CSP Dom. 1627-28,* p. 461; *CSP Dom. 1623-1625*, p. 300

23 *CSP Dom. 1643*, pp. 512-4

24 *Calendar of the Committee for Compounding, 1643-1660 Domestic*, Part 1 p. 299

25 *Calendar of the Committee for the Advance of Money, Domestic, 1642-1656*, Part I, p. 268, p. 49

26 *CCC, 1643-1660* Part 1 pp. 1602-3

27 *CCC, 1643-1660 Domestic*, Part 1 p. 1603

28 *Victoria County History Glos* VI p. 217

29 Joseph Foster, *The register of Admissions to Grays Inn 1521-1889,* 1889, p. 205

30 Edward King, *Old Times Revisited in the Borough and Parish of Lymington*, 1879, 1976 reprint, p. 189

31 HRO 23M54/2 Court Leet and Court Baron of the Manors of Richard Compton, April 1652

32 HRO 12M60/64 A Surveigh of certaine Mannors and Tennements and Farmes Sittuate withn the County of Southampton being parcell of the Possesions of Richard Compton Esq, 1655

33 Rupert Kepple, op. cit., p. 14; HRO Ringwood Baptisms and Burials Registers

34 HRO 12M60/64 A Surveigh...1655, op. cit

35 *The Hampshire Hearth Tax Assessment 1665*, Ed Elizabeth Hughes and Philippa White, Hampshire Record Series Vol XI, Winchester, 1991, p. 64; W. B. Compton, op. cit., p. 72; Nikolaus Pevsner and David Lloyd, *The Buildings of England Hampshire and the Isle of Wight* (1973), p. 110

36 *CCAM, 1642-1656*, Part III, p. 1183; *CSP Dom. 1649-50*, p. 525

37 *CSP Dom. 1650*, pp. 447, 467; *CSP Dom. 1651-52*, pp. 240, 242

38 Debrett's *Peerage, Baronetage, Knightage, and Companionage*, 1921, p. 61; K. G. Ponting, *Wiltshire Portraits*, 1975, Bradford-on-Avon, p. 78

39 *CCAM, 1642-1656*, Part III, p. 1442

40 J.T. Cliffe Ed. *The Cromwellian Decimation Tax of 1655.*, p. 438. in Camden Miscellany XXXIII, 1996

41 HRO QX1/10 Quarter Session Indictments and presentments 1646-1660 Summary with introduction by J. S Furley, 1937, p. 74

42 HRO QX1/3 Index 1658-1672; *Calendar of Treasury Books Vol I 1660-1667*, p. 82

43 W. B. Compton, op. cit., p. 72

44 *Abstract of Claims preferred at a justice seat held for the New Forest in the twenty-second year of the reign of King Charles II. A.D.1670.*, 1853, pp. 232-235; PRO C 99/41 Abstract of Claims 1635, assistance from David Stagg is gratefully acknowledged

45 Percival Lewis, *Historical Inquiries, concerning forests and forest laws, with Topographical Remarks, upon the Ancient and Modern State of the New Forest, in the County of Southampton*, 1811, p. 89

46 PRO C 99/41, Abstract of Claims 1635

47 D J Stagg, *A Calendar of New Forest Documents 15th to 17th centuries*, Hampshire Record Series Vol V, Winchester, 1983, entry numbers 821, 880, 958, 1013, 1084, 1126, 1203, 1249, 1305, 1367, 1420

48 D J Stagg, op. cit., entry numbers 290, 360, 443

2 The Forest Background: Law and Disorder

INTRODUCTION

Forest law is a long and complex subject not yet fully understood. Like common law it was not static but evolved over a period of several centuries. Much of the early workings has enabled scholars to infer the law and the system that was in operation at a particular period. Most of its growth and change occurred between its imposition by the Norman conquerors in the 11th century and the subsequent practical disafforestations that occurred at the commencement of the reign of Edward III (1327). Although its use and relevance waned in subsequent centuries much remained on the statute books until 1971.[1] The New Forest is rich in examples of its continuing usage through to the 19th century. During the early period its purpose was three-fold: to ensure hunting grounds for the king free of interference, to supply meat and to provide revenue.

From the late 14th century onwards there is record, in the New Forest, of a fourth use, with the sale of timber and underwood from coppices.[2] Clearly a much older practice than the date of record (1389), it does indicate a significant pragmatic use of the Forest at a relatively early period. This usage was certainly general in the forests; surveys made nearly 60 years before show coppice workings elsewhere.[3] The succeeding two centuries brought further legislation, mostly of a general nature, that affected use of all the Royal Forests. The most noteworthy statutes indicated a further shift in favour of protecting the vert (specifically the timber) rather than the venison. Although the crown never forgot the revenue value of the forests there appeared to be little tinkering with that side of affairs in the 15th and early 16th century. One statute worth recalling for its impact on private land was made in 1482. This allowed private woods within a forest to be inclosed for up to seven years; in the process it acknowledged that enclosure for three years was customary.[4] The Act for the Preservation of Woods made in 1543 ensured that within coppice enclosures 'standards' were retained thus indicating a requirement for timber as well as the underwood.[5]

NEW FOREST TUDOR ADMINISTRATION

Within the New Forest the administration was in the hands of the Lord Warden appointed by the crown, he had a deputy or Lieutenant. Under them were Foresters or Master Keepers who each looked after a Bailiwick. There were nine of these Bailiwicks, in which the real work was performed by an officer known variously as underkeeper, underforester or groom keeper. His duty was to look after the 'vert and the venison' in order to protect the Monarch's hunting. Burley Bailiwick was the exception with the Forester or Bailiff appointed by the crown. The sovereign also appointed a 'Riding Forester' sometimes known as the Ranger, paid 6d a day, whose duties appeared of a general, though not onerous nature at this time. The previous position of office holders perhaps indicating it was more of a 'pension' than a working post. William Sayntbarbe, appointed in 1553 was a groom of the privy chamber; Edward Creswell, who followed him ten years later was an officer of the Buttery whilst his successor Henry Gifford, was described as 'Queen's servant' in 1576. The appointment was held for life.[6] A deputy riding forester, Jerome Butte, of Brook, yeoman is recorded under Gifford in 1578/9 and 1583.[7]

The remaining officers were appointed, and paid, by the Lord Warden. Two Rangers were chosen to look after the areas known as 'purlieus'. These were adjacent lands, once under forest law but 'disafforested' in the 14th century. The Rangers main job was to drive the deer, which strayed into these areas, back into the Forest. A deputy was employed by both Rangers in the late 1570's chosen from amongst the local yeomanry. The 'Rider' performed a similar job to Agisters or Marksmen overseeing the stock and taking a fee or 'agistment' whilst ensuring that such stock were legally pastured. Forest laws dictated that a Woodward for Minstead was appointed. He had similar duties to an under-keeper protecting the deer and their habitat in private woodlands within a forest. The Lords of the Manor of Minstead took care to insist upon nominating the appointee although he had to swear allegiance to the crown. A Woodward of Ipley is recorded as late as 1537 but may well have disappeared with the uproot-ing of the Abbey at Beaulieu. Two clerical officers, an auditor and a receiver were also in position at this time and, like many of the posts described above, each had a deputy.[8]

ELECTED OFFICERS

Twelve Regarders, elected by the freeholders of the county were to inquire into and report upon 'Articles of the Regard' these essentially being a series of questions as to whether any of the laws of the forest had been broken; they acted as a check upon the foresters or keepers. They made their 'regard' before the forest courts so that the report could be heard there. The Verderers, two in number at this time, also elected by the freeholders of the county were to hear and enrol proceedings at the lower forest courts. These courts were the Wood-mote, sometimes known as the Court of Attachment or Forty day Court (its normal frequency) and the Swainmote. It was left to either the visiting Forest

Eyre, held infrequently if at all in the 16th century, or the deputy justices, to pass sentence.

EXCHEQUER LINKS

Most of the above mentioned posts had been in operation for four hundred years or more and may be traced back to the Charter of the Forest first produced in 1217 or in some cases to the 12th century *Dialogues of the Exchequer* and *Laws of Henry I*. The increasing crown interest in the forests as a reserve for timber meant that new legislation to protect that interest was enacted by the Tudors. As early as 1512 a 'central accounting department for wood sales' was set up which was incorporated into the Court of Surveyors thirty years later.[9] The first major plank in the takeover of the woods came in 1567 when the Justice in Eyre was stripped of his power to make wood sales.[10]

The King's or Queen's Woodward, not to be confused with the individual looking after Minstead or Ipley, had become a key figure by the 16th century. His duty was to assign, fell and sell timber (including lops and tops) either upon receiving an official warrant or as specified in standing instructions. In the New Forest this included timber requirements for fortifications at Portsmouth, Channel Isles, and the Isle of Wight as well as more local use for making pounds, repairing lodges or for fuel assignments. To these ends there was an official axe in use with which it was necessary to mark timber authorised for felling.[11]

PRESERVATORS

As a part of the Exchequer plans for greater productivity around 1567 a new class of officials were set up - 'Preservators'. They were drawn from existing regarders and chosen by the Verderers; two were selected to report on each Bailiwick. As there were nine Bailiwicks and normally twelve Regarders (though fifteen have been recorded in 1488 and 1765) it remains unknown where the rest were drawn from.[12] They were required to answer a series of Articles not unlike the Chapters of the Regard but only including matters directly pertaining to the timber. By 1590 this was refined with six 'chief regarders and preservators' answering the questions and sending their annual report to the Exchequer. These reports, previously referred to elsewhere as 'Regarders Rolls' cover a period of nearly 40 years from 1570 to 1609.[13] Their purpose was to ensure that no wood or timber was taken without their authority; a major part of the work being, as with the regarders, to check upon other crown officials.

The weakness of the system was that, set up by Exchequer warrant, they were obliged to report to the treasury rather than the justice system. All being well between the two departments this should have enabled prosecutions to be made when necessary. In practice there seems to have been friction. The Exchequer chose to use its own court to pursue prosecutions and whilst this did produce some results it was an expensive process not suited to the lesser misdemeanours.[14] It was perhaps, in part, due to this that the misunderstanding arose that forest law had virtually disappeared. Sir William Holdsworth quoted Manwood as pointing 'to the desuetude of the eyre as one of the main causes of the decay of forest law. The desuetude of the eyre meant, in fact, the collapse of the whole system.'[15] In reality this was not the case, the continuance of forest law has been well described elsewhere by David Stagg.[16]

An inquiry of 1609 saw twelve Regarders and six Preservators listed for the New Forest confirming the separation of their roles; its jury recommended that the preservators be dispensed with.[17] Although less is heard of them after this time, they are mentioned in accounts of 1643 and 1648 and again in 1676 and 1684.[18]

After the restoration it seems that little more than lip service was given to the role of preservator. One of the regarders, John Drew, in an inquiry held at Lyndhurst in 1677, stated that although he hadn't been sworn in as a Preservator he signed the account books as one. He describes a system in which in any year three of the Regarders were ordered by the Lord Warden to work with the Woodward thus indicating their abandonment by the Exchequer.[19] By the 18th century they are only known as an historical footnote although the description of the Regarders job in 1789 seems closer to that of the Preservators than their own original purpose.[20]

LATE TUDOR CHANGES

As Queen Elizabeth's reign drew to a close it became obvious that a reform of the administration of the Crown Estates would yield benefits to the nation. Richard Hoyle in *The Estates of the English Crown, 1558-1640* traces that reform to the death of the Lord Treasurer, Burghley and the appointment of his successor, Thomas Sackville, later created earl of Dorset. A combination of increasing land values providing poor returns, combined with fraudulent estate management, was the main criticism held by contemporaries. In any event it was difficult for copyhold income to be improved, where custom ruled, but complaints that fines bore no relation to current values were much easier to prove. One courtier, Sir

Francis Stoner offered to rent the king's woods throughout England for £10,000 per annum more than they brought in.[21]

The complaints against officials in the New Forest are encapsulated in a decree of 1584.[22] In this the Exchequer refers to various proceedings against Keepers, Rangers and Foresters who had taken timber in lieu of wages. It is clear that the process of paying oneself in kind had taken place over a considerable time, 'usurped custome'. Other difficulties are mentioned in that a lease or covenant for 400 acres of land, enclosed for the 'perfecting' of saltpetre, had long since overrun and the work been unsuccessful. A difference had arisen between the Lord Warden, who wanted the use of timber trees in the old park of Lyndhurst to repair and build a lodge in the new park, and those backing the saltpetre developer who wanted to keep the same trees for that use. Saltpetre, the main constituent of gunpowder, whilst not occurring naturally in this country could be manufactured, though the method was not fully appreciated in Elizabethan England. It was decided that the area laid aside should be opened up again.

The same document indicates that the Lord Warden (or his deputy) had previously taken whatever fuel wood he needed, for whilst he now received a generous allowance (50 loads per annum), it was specified that it was to be delivered by the woodward and spent within the Forest. Similarly the keepers had taken a variety of naturally fallen wood and 'inbowes', the latter being branches in which honey was found, instead of fees. The Lord Warden claimed difficulties of paying them their annual fees of 26s 8d because he had lost the benefit of two manors previously held with the Forest. In future each keeper was to have only windfall trees and boughs where no part of the root is showing plus that part of the inbowes on which the bees alight and the honey to be found in the trees. Previously they had evidently felled trees just to obtain the honey. It was also accepted that their wages were inadequate and would be doubled, the money to come from wood sales.

The two rangers and the riding forester had previously taken nine loads of wood from each Bailiwick. In lieu of this they were to receive £4 per annum apart from the riding forester who was to have £5, because of his greater travelling; the money to be raised by wood sales. The nine keepers had fuel for use in their lodges, they were now to receive twelve loads per annum delivered to them by the Queen's woodward.

The stock pounds that were used in the drifts of the Forest had been 'over engineered' for whole trees seem to have been used prior to the decree. Thereafter only cleft and sawn timber was to be used in their construction. The drifts were noted as being for the cattle and hogs - an indication of the predominance of these two animals at that time. A concern of the Lord Warden was that those dwelling in 'newe builded and erected Cottagies within the saide Forreste' were taking wood for their cottages. A retrospective restriction was placed on them by forbidding any inhabitant dwelling in such a house, built since the beginning of the Queen's reign, from taking wood.

In summary it may be stated that the problems arose from officers helping themselves in the absence of (adequate) pay and the pressures of new industry and 'incomers'. The problems were not all solved at a stroke by the decree for it failed to address the opportunities that were available for corrupt dealings in the hands of pernicious officers.

The Preservators reports described above attest to the need for the decree. The record of the following years show all working well with the correct allotment of fuel to the keepers, hog and cattle pounds being made, a note of who timber was sold to. However within six years some of the old habits were creeping back in: 'John Tucher the keeper cut certain green boughs' and 'Edmond Browne of Brockenhurst, unlawful wood to his house' being examples.[23] The system clearly didn't work as intended; James Reynolds, keeper of the Inn (Lyndhurst) Bailiwick figured in the early lists of transgressors felling timber without warrant. By 1591 he had become a Preservator and within six years had been accused, with others, of detaining 'the profits' of the Forest.[24] Little wonder that the office of preservator failed to survive.

EXCHEQUER ABUSES

It might be thought from the above that all the fault lay on the side of the officers under the Lord Warden. A document in the Land Revenue filed by Henry Campion, Surveyor of Lands and Revenues for the county of Southampton, made around 1598, shows that that was not the case. The report, addressed to the Queen, shows exasperation with the activities of the Woodwards over a period of years. Campion commences by quoting the case of Arthur Swayne, appointed Woodward in 1588 at an annual fee of £5, of unwarranted felling of timber worth £200, of accounting for just £20 of the proceeds to the Exchequer and his obtaining 23 shillings a piece for 46 of the trees sold to Phillip Stride. He goes on to accuse Swayne with John Vine of Lyndhurst, and others, of more misdeeds before selling his appointment to Henry Audly for £300, six years later. As his appointment was by Letters Patent he had to arrange for a suitable successor to be recommended. This he found in the delightfully named William Christmas who he claimed was appointed in name only and was to work with an assistant William Osland, a servant of, and both to be under the direction of, Henry Audly. Another half a dozen people were indicted by Campion including the Surveyor John Taverner.[25]

Upon those accused finding out they were being investigated they combined and procured a commission, held at Romsey, which they were able to manipulate by packing the jury with friends. There is some corroboration of Campion's evidence in the Preservators reports of the 1590's, though strangely there are gaps or very brief entries for 1591-3, the precise time when the misdemeanours are said to have taken place. Campion's appeal seems to have fallen on deaf ears, Vine retained the benefit of a grant of crown lands in 1604 whilst Christmas still held his post in 1622.[26]

CHANGE

With the arrival of a new king, James I, keen on hunting, measures were taken to ensure that the forest laws were upheld. Some commentators have seen this interest in the forest as a revival of forest law. Whilst it is true that the Tudors had less interest in hunting than James they had no wish to let lapse a system which provided them with income. James was not slow to listen to contemporaries who advised him of waste and poor returns on crown lands.

In an important article on the state of forest laws under Charles I George Hammersley puts the case that the laws were 'still widely known and respected'. After expounding the system in use he concludes that:-

> There were always two sides to the forest laws: they punished and restricted, it is true, but they also maintained securely a system of husbandry well suited to the extensive exploitation of rough woodland and waste.

He went on to say that 'those who were compelled to live under the forest law had come to regard it as beneficial'.[27]

Change could only occur where the crown decided that its use for hunting was no longer prime and this was not immediately the case. However the seeds of change had been sown a century before with the institution of a wood sales department. In the early years of the 17th century it was necessary to clarify the situation as to who had authority to remove wood or timber from the forest. Both those concerned with protecting the vert for the King's pleasure and those looking after it for his profit had greatly differing priorities. A compromise between the Justice in Eyre, the earl of Nottingham, and the Lord Treasurer, the earl of Dorset, was reached, in 1606, ensuring that neither department could act without advising and in some cases obtaining the permission of the other in the matter of felling timber and other wood.[28]

In the first decade of the new century a string of inquiries, surveys, and inquisitions took place within the Forest with a view to not just improving the situation, as had happened twenty years before, but radically improving it for revenue. These were meant to be long term measures and with that in mind the expense of the surveys both written and mapped, although quite high, was justifiable.[29] Warrants, issued in February and March 1608 to the Woodward of the New Forest, William Christmas, for erecting five new lodges indicate a major change of policy.[30] An undated inquiry which reported c 1609 records the Bailiwicks with their officers and lodges. With the exception of Godshill and Linwood there was to be two lodges to each area with two or three underkeepers. This may be the stage at which the term 'Walk' comes into common usage; although sixty years later it was still used for Bailiwick rather than the subdivision it came to mean in the 18th century.[31] At the same time a series of grants of land was begun, the first completed in December 1608, resulted in income of £1015 19s, three more the following May and June totalled £1552 6s 4d. Further, lower valued grants followed in 1613 and 1631. The lands involved, though not always described as such, appear to be ssarts (forest made arable) and purprestures (encroachments). They were not necessarily of recent date and may have been granted and re-granted a number of times. It was presumably left for the occupiers of these lands to bargain with the grantees for rent or purchase.[32] Most of the land at Minstead between 'Golden Croft' and 'Duell's Farm' near Football Green was contained in one of these grants known as 'Chamberlains Patent' in 1631.[33]

1635 CLAIMS and CIVIL UNREST

The 1635 claims were probably called for with a view to a sale of the Forest. Both James I and Charles I had sought new means of raising money, the latter often without the aid of parliament. Leases of coppices and grants of office were traditional means of yielding profits in the forests. In the first half of the century the sale of the forests themselves rather than the timber or underwood was proposed by various revenue commissions.[34] It was probably only on account of more pressing problems elsewhere that this did not occur; change in the Forest is rarely a quick process.

The claims themselves present some interesting reading for the list includes four men who believed that their office gave them a right to claim: Woodward Gabriel Lapp, Riding Forester Cuthbert Bacon, the Bailiff of Burley the earl of Pembroke and for the Lord Warden's post the earl of Southampton. Perhaps the oddest one is the claim of John Chamberlain for various purprestures totalling 120 acres. These were the subject of a grant to him in 1631 and whilst they may not all have been recent encroachments it seems incongruous that as such they could qualify for rights of common.[35] In 1643 Charles I raised over £27,000 by granting to trustees not only the New Forest but also Sherwood, Clarendon and Bowood Parks amongst other lands. The trustees received little benefit from their action, despite pleas to Charles II at the restoration, most ended up close to bankruptcy.[36]

Taken over by Cromwell and the Commonwealth, plans to sell off virtually all of the Royal Forests were made in the 1650's. Surveys were undertaken and valuations produced. Seven forests, including the New Forest, were held in reserve but then four more of these were added into the sale plans. The New Forest was one of the three not taken up, Dean and a 'forest on the Isle of Wight' were the other two.[37] The situation must have been of great concern locally and naturally there were other plans to exploit the area. Amongst the lesser known sources of revenue was the granting of permission for a coal mine in 1653, and the new Decoy Pond near Beaulieu Road. The former, presumably minehouse grounds near Lyndhurst, was a privately funded operation with the crown taking an eighth of the profits.[38]

RESTORATION and the LAST FOREST EYRE

After the restoration the newly revived forest courts record a number of the same, relatively minor offences as pre-war, many involving forest officers. Some received heavy penalties and perhaps shows the continuing difficulties of the division between the Lord Wardens officers and those of the Exchequer. The Keepers (not for the first time, nor for the last) were charged with taking excessive wood under excuse of using it for browse wood for the deer.[39]

At the last Forest Eyre held in the New Forest in 1670 an extensive enquiry was made as to conditions in the Forest.[40] As in 1635 claims were received though this time they were entered by a greater number of the inhabitants; 308 as against 244. This wasn't just a case of land being split or more encroachers claiming rights. Claims in Minstead in 1635 were by just four individuals. Sir Henry Compton claimed for himself and his tenants within the Manor, Melior Lovell for 2 messuages and 46 acres, Robert Morrice for a messuage and 3 acres and John Chater for a messuage and 8 acres at London Minstead.[41] None of the tenants of Lyndhurst Manor are included nor are a number of others whose rights were not questioned. Those who were listed at London Minstead as freeholders in 1635 but not in the claims were Richard Goddard, arm., Francis Rainger, John Crowcher, John Roberts gent.[42] Whether it was deliberately made difficult to apply, or potential claimants were concerned about losing their land by the earlier grants, is not known. Much has been written about the proceedings of the Forest Eyres under Finch together with his authoritarian methods.

In 1670 six tenants of Lyndhurst Manor claim for holdings at London Minstead together with three other freeholders and a further six in Minstead apart from the claim of Richard Compton on behalf of himself and his tenants for Minstead Manor. The form of claim seems to have changed little in the 35 years. John Chater's 1635 claim, made by his attorney Edward Offley, is virtually identical to that put in on his son's behalf by Anthony Clapshawe in 1670. Again the claim of Richard Compton is very similar to that made by his father Sir Henry. The main matters as concerns forest rights and his claim of pasture by vicinage is the same. A notable difference is that in 1670 he claims the right to hold his courts, the view of frankpledge and the court baron with those matters pertaining to them without adding the detail. In 1635 he specifies 'fines and corrections with pillory and tumbrel... assize of bread and ale...waifs and strays'.[43]

The 1670 Eyre seems to show the way matters are moving with explicit attempts to control the power of the keepers. This is further borne out by a number of inquistions held in the succeeding twenty years.

WASTES and SPOILS

The treasury books are full of inquiries to be made into 'wastes and spoils' of the New Forest in the 1670's, 80's and 90's.[44] Rather like the poor law, the fact that there were so many attempts makes it clear that no effective remedy was found for a considerable time. Some provide vivid detail not only of the administration but also of the uses to which the inhabitants put the Forest and its products. The waste believed to be occasioned by those having no right to fuel wood or exceeding their right was of prime concern in all these inquiries.

By the end of this period the question is being addressed as to whether those entitled should have the fuel wood assigned to them by officers of the crown or should be allowed to take it at their liberty. The difficulties of the former method were clear for the officers themselves were amassing vast amounts of wood, some under pretence of cutting browse for the deer, others by over supply of fuel wood.[45] Contradictory conclusions were reached as to the best method of dealing with the problem. One inquiry insisted that the then current method of assignment wasn't working and that it would be better to return to the old way of those entitled collecting their own fuel wood.

The allotment of wood for fuel to the lodges decreed by Elizabeth I ninety years before still held. An inquiry of 1677 gives some detail of the method of allocation for commoners both then and earlier. John Elcombe, a tenant of Lyndhurst Manor, stated that by custom the thirty two tenants had fuel wood by 'Hooke and Crooke onely'. He went on to claim that they were the only ones entitled to such fuel and that other freeholders of the Forest who claimed it in 1670 were not entitled to it.[46] The fuel wood was one of a number of rights that such tenants might enjoy, these included wood for the repair of their houses, hedges and ploughs, it being implicit that it was for use on the copyhold and for the direct benefit of the copyholder only.[47]

Numerous abuses by officials deposed in the inquistions of this period provide evidence not only of the depredations made but also of the difficulties encountered by those who refused to turn a blind eye. Drew Penton made a statement to the 1677 inquiry in which he accused the keeper of Castle Malwood Lodge, John Cary, of taking good timber trees for his own use both for sale and as fuel wood (without assignment). He stated that 'he had known the said walke and the woods in it above these twenty yeares liveing in and neere to the same And yt[that] he believed there had beene more spoiles and abuses and more wood and tymber cutt in three yeares (vizt in the yeare 1671:1672:and 1673)'. Abuses of 'lops and tops' and browse wood far too large for deer, a 'foote over' were also stated. In opening his deposition on 20th August Penton claimed that he had not come forward at the previous commission 'because the Keepers putt a terror on him'. He was dead by the following spring.[48]

The reports that came out of this and other inquiries highlighted the problems, showing that abuses by the officers provided examples that the inhabitants followed. One report after detailing the particular troubles and potential remedies encapsulated the real problem in its ultimate paragraph:-

That a greate cause why there are soe many abuses and spoiles comit-
ted and donne w[i]thin the Forest is because that justice is not speedily
executed upon offenders by means wherof they thinke themselve secure
and makes them p[re]sume to doe greate mischiefs then other wise they
would.[49]

ENCLOSURE

As early as 1669 serious attempts were made to enclose 1000 acres in each walk
of the Forest.[50] The plan was embarked upon but unsuccessful. The, by now,
old differences between Exchequer and Justices show in that a hundred acre
enclosure made at Holm Hill was recorded as an offence against forest law by
the Regarders in 1670.[51] The enclosure bank was substantial, over six feet high,
but thrown down and cattle allowed in.[52] It was clear that there was little chance
of success for such a scheme without parliamentary assistance despite a move in
the country as a whole to 'improve' the waste lands through enclosure. The bill
for the 1698 Act engendered a great deal of opposition from those who saw their
rights disappearing. Landowners and their tenants, numbering over a thousand,
petitioned parliament but to little avail.

1698 ACT

It was not until a statute was enacted in 1698 (after an aborted effort in 1692)
that a serious endeavour was made to reconcile the various interests and develop
the Forest systematically for its timber growing potential.[53]

The statute has an eye to the future but, like most, reflects on past problems.
Rather than continue to try and obtain naval timber from the open forest it was
decided that the best solution was enclosure. It was necessary to spell out that
the enclosure was for the sole purpose of timber and not for corn or cattle to
graze; clearly procedures that had happened in earlier attempts. Common rights
were to be suspended over the land for as long as it was enclosed. It was specifically stated that forest officers were to be fined and sacked for allowing a
variety of misuses of oak and beech trees. They were also charged with ensuring
that charcoal making didn't occur inside or within a thousand paces of the new
enclosures. Charcoal making was to be regulated with sites approved by forest
officers and an appropriate type of fencing (heather and furze) used. Illegal
grazing was a problem too, for the keepers were required to make drifts of the
Forest as they had in earlier times.[54]

A carrot and stick approach was taken with the resident populace. In anticipation of local difficulties penalties were included for fence breaking and general damage. Fines were to be imposed with a reward being offered for informers. This perhaps recalls the problems in the Forest of Dean after the Act of 1666.[55] However, and importantly, this Act also recognized the commoners pasture and pannage rights together with other privileges including fuel rights though with some limitations as to the season.

Further confirmation of earlier difficulties was in an assurance that no individuals were to have an interest in enclosures, woods or wastelands or woods or trees growing upon them. Gifts and grants of a variety of benefits had been the rule throughout the century. '...the said Forest may be perpetually estated and preserved in the Crown for publick Use...'[56] Some rather odd dealings had occurred when wood sales had taken place, this was to be remedied by advertising the sales and stipulating a minimum price.

Four of the thirteen sections of the Act were specifically targeted at forest officers.[57] Their misuse of the Forest in combination with others (such as charcoal makers) was implied in three others.[58]

It may be summarised that, whilst many of the problems that occurred were caused by officers being rather generous in looking after their own interests, this was in many ways matched by the inhabitants doing the same. Undoubtedly the most important change was the legal confirmation of the previously tacit rights of commoners and their use of the Forest for their own industry. It was no longer a place disputed by two arms of the nation for hunting and shipbuilding, but a third force, commoning, always present but previously with little power and no protection, was now able to have its say.

Notes

1   Eliz. II, 1971 c. 47, Wild Creatures and Forest Laws Act
2   C. R. Tubbs, *The New Forest*, 1986, p 73
3   The Forests by Nellie Neilson in *The English Government at Work 1327-1336* vol.1, 1940 Edited by James F. Willard & William A. Morris, pp. 427-8
4   Statute 22 Edw. 4. c. 7
5   Statute 35 Hen. VIII c. 17
6   *CPR* 3rd July 1553; 25th Jan 1563; 2nd April 1576; Gifford, who lived at Kings Somborne and had good connections to important Hampshire families used them to secure election as MP for Stockbridge, died in 1592. 'He made no mark on the

records of the House of Commons, and little elsewhere' - P W Hasler *The House of Commons 1558-1603* vol II p. 190

7   PRO E 101/142/16, m 6; PRO E 101/142/17, m 4

8   D J Stagg, The Orders and Rules of the New Forest AD 1537, *HFC New Forest Section Report 13*, 1974; PRO E 101/142/16, 'Regarders Certificates'

9   G. Hammersley in The Crown Woods and their Exploitation in the 16/17th centuries, *Bull. Inst. Hist. Research*, 30, 1957, p. 137; 33 Hen. 8 c. 39

10   R Hoyle Ed., *The Estates of the English Crown 1558-1640*, 1992, p. 356

11   PRO E 178/3097 m 34; *Cal Treas Bks* 13 Dec 1676; HRO 149M89/R5/6457A Bedford Papers, Accounts - purchase of Axe

12   Stagg, 1983, op. cit., 88; HRO 149M89/R4/6145, Samber Mss; See also P. Roberts, Elizabethan Conservators of the New Forest, *Hampshire Studies 2001 V*ol 56, pp. 246-253

13   P A J Pettit, *The Royal Forests of Northamptonshire 1558-1714*, Northants Record Society, 1968 pp. 28-31. Appendix III; PRO E 101/142/12-20, E 101/536/30-32, E 101/536/34-35, E 101/143/1, E 178/3097 mm 55-7

14   Pettit, op. cit., p. 30

15   Sir William Holdsworth, *A History of English Law*, 7th Edition vol 1, p. 104

16   Stagg, 1983, op. cit., xv-xxxiv

17   PRO E 178/3097

18   PRO CRES2/1673; *Cal Treas Bks* 13 Dec 1676; PRO LR9 15/558

19   PRO E 178/6453, 31st August 1677

20   HRO 149M89/R4/6145, Samber mss of 1765 p. 6; 5th Report, 1789 app 7, app 12

21   *CSP Dom. 1603-1610*, p. 388 Dec 1607

22   Decree of Court of Exchequer 26 Eliz 19th June, *Fifth Report of the Commissioners appointed to enquire into the State and Conditions of the Woods, Forests, and Land Revenues of the Crown*, 22 July 1789, pp. 51-2

23   PRO E 101/142/19, m 2, South Bailiwick

24   *CSP Dom.* 1595/7, 24th Jan 1597 p. 351

25   PRO LR 2/266, mm 26-27

26   PRO SP Dom, Jas I. Vol. 8, No. 76; Lyndhurst, 1604 Survey of the Manor; Stagg, 1983, op. cit., Appendix B

27   G Hammersley, The Revival of the Forest laws under Charles I, *History*, 45, 1960, pp. 86-7

28   Coke *4th Institute* pp. 299-300 The Court of the Forest

29   Hoyle, op. cit. pp. 220-3

30   *CSP Dom 1603-10* p. 408

31   PRO E 178/3097, mm 25-26

32   Stagg, 1983, op. cit., 1559, 1597, 1659, 1668 and 1671

33   HRO 81M74/48, Abstract of title of Duells Farm from 1700

34   G. Hammersley, 1957, op. cit. p. 158

35   PRO C 99/41, no 183

36   *Cal Treasury Books, vol.I, 47* (17 Dec 1660); B D Henning, *History of Parliament, The House of Commons 1660-90*, 1983; *DNB*

37 Firth and Rait, *Acts and Ordinances of the Interregnum*, 1911, 3 vols, vol II pp. 783, 811

38 *CSP Dom*. Dec 1653; PRO F 20/48, Abraham and William Driver, Survey of Castle Malwood, 1787; GR SU3007; Stagg, 1983, op. cit., 1555

39 Stagg, 1983, op. cit., 908-917

40 *Claims*, 1670, op. cit.

41 PRO C 99/41, nos 1, 23, 118, 187

42 Stagg, 1983, op. cit., 453

43 PRO C 99/41, no 1

44 *CTB* 11 Mar 1672; *CTB* 28th April 1673; *CTB* 16th Aug 1676; *CTB* 20th Dec 1676; *CTB* 2nd Sept 1679; *CTB* 9th Nov 1686; *CTP* 17th Feb 1691; *CTB* 16th Mar 1692; *CTB* 1st June 1693; *CTP* 11th July 1694

45 HRO 1688A092/1-2 Inventory and account of Arthur Oxford, an underkeeper, is an interesting example

46 PRO E 178/6453, Lyndhurst 14th August; 31 tenants are listed in the 1670 claims but see note in HRO 149M89/R4/6137

47 A series of appendices relating to fuel rights in a report made by Lord Glenbervie in 1804 together with a list recently come to light comparing fuel rights of Lynd-hurst Manor tenants in 1670 and 1752, have helped establish property positions and occupiers and owners in London Minstead. Caution is needed for the Glenbervie 1670 claims are based on the inaccurate 1776 anonymous publication (now thought to be compiled by William Samber). The same could now be done with other properties in Bartley and Lyndhurst. PRO F 20/52 Report of Lord Glenbervie to the Lords of the Treasury 19th dec 1804; HRO 149M89/R4/6137

48 PRO E 178/6453, Inquiry into wastes and spoiles of the New Forest, Brook 20th August 1677; HRO 1677AD89

49 PRO E 178/6453

50 *CTB*, 12 Oct 1669

51 Stagg, 1983, op. cit., 1555

52 Historical Manuscripts Commission *Calendar of the House of Lords Manuscripts 1678-1714*, 14 vols, 1887-1953, 1698, no. 1255, p. 190

53 Journal House of Commons Vol 10 p. 773 9th Jan 1692, A Bill for the 'Increase and preservation of Timber in the New Forest in the county of Southampton'

54 Statute 9 & 10 Will. III, c.36, An Act for the Increase and Preservation of the Timber in the New Forest, AD 1698; Statute 32 Hen. VIII c 13

55 C.E. Hart, *Royal Forest*, Oxford 1966 p. 171

56 Statute 9 & 10 Will. III, c.36, s 10

57 Statute 9 & 10 Will. III, c.36, s 5, 11, 12 and 13

58 Statute 9 & 10 Will. III, c.36, s 3, 4, 10

3 Land: Rights and Regulations

INTRODUCTION

Most of the occupied land in the 17th century was held by the Compton family as the Manor of Minstead. Two hundred and forty seven acres were enclosed within the manor in 1655. The system of administration that was in use there affected the other land holders so this will be described first. In 1670 there was at least a further two hundred and eleven acres shared between the Crown Manor of Lyndhurst and freeholders on the eastern side of the parish. In addition to this there may have been others, possibly recent encroachers, who did not wish to draw attention to themselves by making a claim for forest rights or who missed the opportunity.[1]

MANORIAL COURTS and THE LAW

The administration of the lands of the Comptons was through regularly held courts, not unlike the Verderer's courts which are held to this day in Lyndhurst. Unfortunately records only survive, in the period under consideration, for the years 1652-6 and 1690-1706. The later Court is primarily concerned with the transfer of land. There is much greater detail of the running of the manor for the earlier period and it is that which will be discussed here. Two distinct manorial courts were held in Minstead in the 1650's. The View of Frankpledge, also known as a Court Leet, dealt with minor criminal matters. The Court Baron was concerned with the domestic running of the manor including customs and changes in land holdings. The name Frankpledge originated from the freemen who pledged themselves together for their mutual good behaviour.[2]

Fig 6 Manor Boundary Bank near Ringwood Ford

The jurisdiction of the Courts applied not only to the Manorial tenants, but also to the freeholders whose attendance was required as well as others passing through the manor. For this purpose it was necessary that all should know when they were within the manor. A series of boundary cairns, stones or mounds were used at suitable entry points. Three or possibly four 'gates' were still known in the latter half of the 16th century though only one is still in common usage at Pilmore Gate Heath.[3] Beaulieu still retains these obvious markers on its boundaries.

The steward's duty was to hold these courts; he would have controlled their frequency and form subject to the laws of the land. During the years 1652-4 the courts, both Baron and Frankpledge which were held on the same day, took place in April and October. It would appear that the Court Baron was held first. The power and duties of these courts had been gradually eroded following the Tudor changes to the administration of law through the parishes and Justices of the Peace. This continued through the Interregnum with the need for just one court day in both 1655 and 1656. The allegiance of the Jury of the Court, which was made up of local men, was altered from 'the Keepers of the Liberty of England' to 'the Lord Protector' in 1654 following the instigation of the Protectorate in 1653.

MANORIAL CUSTOMS

The first court baron, in April 1652, provides not only a roll call of residents and their status but also a note of the customs of the manor. It is apparent that this is the first held in Minstead under Richard Compton, for the initial task of the steward was to establish the practice there. The homage (jury) are sworn and state their case upon oath.

The Lord could grant any customary or copyhold tenements and lands by copy for one life in possession and two in reversion and that the widow of any dying in possession should hold the tenancy during her widowhood.

Every customary tenant had the right to take upon their lands 'hedgeboote ploughboote and cartboote'. This is the right to take wood for the purposes of making or repairing hedges, ploughs and carts. Within the Forest the common of estovers is the nearest equivalent to it, though restrictions on its use have become muddled and lost over time. In manorial custom it usually encompassed 'houseboote' the right to take wood for repair or building of houses - that is a surprising omission but may well reflect the position of the Manor within the Forest. However it is clear from the courts that timber was assigned for this purpose - indeed it was a common complaint that the 'tenement of' so and so 'was in decay and needed repair'.

The tenants had the right to purchase their possession at a penny less than the 'going rate'. This custom, which was not exercised at this time, is of limited benefit, for only the larger farmers with other freehold property would have been likely to afford their tenancy. It would be interesting to know if it was invoked in 1921 when many of the holdings of the manor were sold.

The right of common of turbary was exercised and guarded. Concern at tenants who had erected cottages on the common being allowed to cut turf was evinced to the extent of an Elizabethan statute being quoted, which forbade the construction of cottages on the waste without four acres of land attached.[4] The court stated that the customary tenants were allowed turf at 3s 4d per thousand. Two years later it became necessary to limit this to a maximum of 4,000 turves per year for each customary tenant and to allow 2,000 a year to the cottagers. This may have been an oversight on the part of the jurors in 1652 or a ploy to deliberately mislead the new Landlord or a reaction to increased housing pressure. Further constraints were made in October 1655 when only cottagers who were lease holders of the manor were allowed their two thousand turves. Beyond that the lease holders paid 10s a thousand as did those cottagers without leases for any turves they dug. Whether this was intended to be an economic exercise for the benefit of the lord of the manor or a control because of an increasing problem is unclear although the latter seems more likely. The number of turves allowed to be taken per annum was identical to that quoted in 1875 for those with similar rights over the Forest.[5]

Custom is the word that runs throughout the court baron records. Whenever property changes hands - and that is one of the most important purposes of the court - the word crops up. A typical example:-

> First they p[re]sent That Thomas Freind who held by Copy of Court Roll dated the twelvth day of October In the Seaventeenth yeare of the Raigne of our late Sov[er]aigne Lord King James One Close called Mill Close contayning Four acres within the mannor aforesaid for Tearme of his life according to the Custome of the said Mannor is dead Since the last Court whereupon there happeneth to the Lord for a herriott One Colt already seized to the use of the Lord by John Call and Edmund Waters his Offic-ers, and delive[r]ed at Bisterne by Henry Curtis to the Lord aforesaid; And that Thomas Martin is next Ten[a]nte and ought to be admitted hereto, for his life according to the Custome of the Mannor aforesaid....[6]

The importance of all the tenants and freeholders knowing the 'Limittes and boundes of their Liberte and Mannor' was achieved by walking the boundary.

Fig 7 **Manor Boundary Stone at Seamans Corner**

On Whit Monday 1653 the entire village met at Seamans Corner to view the boundary and set marks at appropriate places. The practice of marking continued into the 19th century for the stones that are now to be seen are cut with the letters 'HCC' for Henry Combe Compton, who was Lord of the manor from 1803 until his death in 1866.[7] One on the green at Seamans corner is still easily seen though there are a number dividing the waste or common land from the forest and along Silver Street at Emery Down. The manorial courts were operated under statute law and although many of the customs were local ones, obedience of the national law took precedence.

MANOR OFFICIALS

Francis Sambrooke appeared, from the records that are extant, to have been an able steward. He was probably the son of one Francis Sambrooke, a Tailor of Salisbury.[8] What happened to the records of the courts held between 1656 and 1690 is not known.[9] Sambrooke's predecessor as Steward of the Compton estates was Richard Goddard who also held the same post in the New Forest before and after the civil war.[10]

Although in former times and other Manors the steward's duty included overseeing the running of communal agriculture this applied little to Minstead. No record of common fields has been found and therefore there was no manorial plough or plough teams to organise. The evidence of the surviving inventories show that the ploughs that existed were held privately. Although no appointment of a reeve has been found in these records, one was required, and did appear at forest courts in 1635 and the 1660's.[11] He acted as a spokesperson representing the vill or hamlet at the forest courts; Minstead made one appointment whilst London Minstead combined with Bartley Regis for another. A bailiff, Henry Curtis, was appointed in the April 1653 Court Baron; his duties included collecting arrears of rents and fines. He was also required to seize the appropriate beast when due for a heriot (fine on death of a copyholder) as well as impound and keep (for the lord of the Manor) 'Felons goodes waifes and strayes'. Curtis's position as bailiff working for the Lord seems to be in some conflict with his duties as a hayward, a position he was appointed to in the same year whereby he was required to look after the common pasturage. He evidently carried out those duties for he is paid by the churchwardens for watching 'Lambs and beast 1[s] 3[d]'.[12] That many duties of the manorial officers were being taken over by the parish is clear, for at the same time one of the churchwardens, Phillip Ansell, paid himself as well as Curtis for watching lambs. There were other duties attached to the post of Hayward, for in 1655 he was required to impound any pigs found without rings.[13] In former times the hayward would have been responsible for seeing that the tenants performed the manorial work required of them and more general duties in protecting the crops and produce of the manor.[14] Details of impounding of strays is given on a couple of occasions. The first when William Wakeford was fined 1s for breaking the pound on 19th September 1654 to release four heifers. The second offender, a year later was Lyndhurst blacksmith, John Rasbridge, (his name lived on in the lane in Lyndhurst) who broke the pound and took away six heifers on 10th September.[15]

The affeerers' duty was to assess amercements (penalties) for those offences where a fine or penalty was not specified by statute. The same people officiated in both courts, Baron and Frankpledge. On occasions the whole homage affeered a particular item such as occurred in the October 1653 Baron when it was considered that a barn had been illegally erected on the common by Edward White and also in October 1656 when the dwelling of Richard Read was declared in decay and in need of a ton and half of timber for repairs.

LAW and ORDER

The Tithingman, who as parish constable, had the general duty of preserving the peace, was regularly appointed, usually for a year. It was not always a popular job with the incumbent's neighbours. There appears to be some overlapping with the parish officers. Although the vestry records do not record the separate appointment of a constable the churchwardens' duties seem to include this. Phillip Ansell not only claimed expenses for fetching a warrant for 'Bidlecome' but also 'for goeing after John Bidlecombe...' whilst he was a warden in 1653.

Robert Lamb held the post until April 1652, his successors as Tithingmen were Edward White jnr and John Burden who was replaced after only six months. William Olding completed his term plus a further six months and was followed by John Henbest, Thomas Blake the elder and James Phillips. Olding seemed to have the most to cope with, apprehending two strangers, Phillip Goldstone and John Hartgill, suspected of felony and robbery.[16] As amongst the items found on them were three pistols and a rapier, their arrest must have required some courage. They were taken before a magistrate, Henry Bromfield of Boldre - one of the few to serve under both Carolian Kings and during the Commonwealth period - who committed them to the county gaol at Winchester. At the follow-ing Assizes before Justice Henry Rolle, Goldstone was convicted of felony and burned in the hand whilst Hartgill was found not guilty, released and had his goods restored to him.[17] In general the lack of reports in the manorial courts suggest that many of the policing duties within the area were carried out by appointees of the Vestry Court. Justice Rolle was one of the two Judges appre-hended by John Penruddock in the uprising at Salisbury the following year and threatened with hanging by his compatriot, Wagstaffe.

Many of the appointments made by manor courts were no longer necessary as the homage or jury consisted of local men who made presentments on par-ticular problems, not unlike the present Verderers Court where anybody may make a presentment that concerns the Forest. The scouring of ditches was a regular request at the courts - there was no need to appoint a separate surveyor of hedges, ditches and watercourses. Other posts such as ale-tasters had been transferred to the jurisdiction of the quarter sessions. Unlicensed alehouses were in evidence after the civil war no doubt due to the lax or non-existent administration of that time.[18]

It was to be expected that the Court of the View of Frankpledge would be mostly concerned with minor offences but there is some cross over between the two courts particularly in the case of those presented with failing to keep their ditches clear. There were five occasions when this was bought up in the Frank-pledge or Leet Court. Although the phrasing is sometimes quaint to the modern reader 'The water being stopt and the highway therby annoyed' the meaning is clear. Whilst some items concerned the community as a whole, such as the necessity to ensure that the stocks were kept in good order, others were very much to do with individual behaviour. James Phillips was fined five shillings for being drunk and disorderly in court in April 1653. It is interesting to note that this did not debar him from duty as Tithingman three years later. Some items sound harsh; George Howse had taken in a poor woman, a widow by the name of Ratway, he was ordered to remove her though given six months to do so.[19] Richard Osmund was fined a shilling for non appearance at the court although 'living within the precinct of this Court'. It had been noted that a cottage built by Osmund was within the manor and 'not without as he pretended'.[20] He is probably the same Richard Osman who enclosed 20 perch of the king's desmesne 20 years before and 'built a dwelling house where no house was previously'.[21]

MANOR CUSTOMS - CONCLUSIONS

Minstead customs were expressed by the court as a whole 'it is the custom ...' This reflects the basic system of self government that was in existence not only in feudal times but also for some centuries before.[22] It is clear that although there might be orders given there still has to be the consent of the court to matters that affect the community as a whole. An example would be the enclosure of land for the windmill - this being for the general benefit of the manor. Although the village seemed to accept some of the squatters on the common there were objections to them in specific instances - their right of turbary being one. The manorial records indicate that there must already have been problems with damage to the waste through over use of this right by the commoners and that some limitation was due. Equally well if a manorial tenant misused the waste he had to answer to the court. Edward White, referred to earlier, was not the only tenant who encroached onto the common. Richard Masy was presented for this offence and given until the end of the following month to lay the land open and 'levell the Fence'. At the same court Robert Whitehorne was charged with exactly the same offence but given until the following May to restore the land.[23]

What is particularly interesting is to see the number of occasions that the court made a presentment concerning an individual's tenement or barn. There are a total of forty nine dwellings listed in a survey of the manor made in 1655, seventeen of which were at some point in the years 1652-6 considered in need of repair. The urgency of the repair is clearly expressed in that, in the event of non-repair, there is either to be a fine of 10s or forfeiture. This would seem to be a reflection on the weak structure and impermanence of many buildings. Those that have survived from that time in the village are clearly quite substantial with timber frames and brick infill and likely to have been part of the more substantial 'homesteds' noted in the survey. There is also concern for barns with three requiring repairs. This appears to reflect a need to maintain property for the well being of the community as a unit, with a thought for how any potential loss would affect tenants present or future children. Similarly the reason for a number of presentments concerning scouring of ditches is clear with backup of water onto fields affecting the community at large.

Virtually all the stock kept by inhabitants was of the kind commonable to a forest. No mention is made of geese, only one person had goats and he was a forest officer at Bolderwood, though a few, six, did keep sheep. Even so the numbers are very low reflecting the lack of sheep rights in the area. Pigs were kept by a large proportion of the inhabitants, although not commonable on the forest except during the pannage season (common of mast). It would seem by an order of the Court Baron made in the autumn of 1655 for the ringing of pigs that the same rules applied in Minstead Manor as did on the Forest.

Another interesting reminder of forest law is in the replacement timber required for repairing property. Tenants were only allotted wood if there was any growing on their copyhold. This would seem to indicate a strict observance of forest law at a relatively late date. There is of course the often quoted claim made in 1670 by the lord of the manor, Richard Compton, of rights of common of pasture and mast by vicinage 'without paying anything therefore'. The claim acknowledges that vicinage is a two way process and goes on, rather cheekily, to state that the King has similar rights for his commonable animals 'in the wastes and woods of the soil of the said Richard, on account of vicinage, Without paying anything therefore'. Far more is claimed including the right of entry and exit to and from the Forest, as well as for Richard Compton and his heirs to hold his manorial courts within the manor twice yearly.[24] The waste lands of Minstead directly abut, and are totally surrounded by, the Crown lands. Neither area is (or can be without statute) enclosed, so livestock were, and are, free to roam between the two without let or hindrance. A similar claim of intercommoning was made in the same century by inhabitants of villages adjacent to a Royal Forest in Northamptonshire.[25]

Fig 8 **The Manor waste and Forest are contiguous. The ponies are on the Manor, the photographer on the Forest**

From this it will be seen that Minstead Manor was not only under forest law but that its own rights and customs were, if not identical with, then, closely allied with those of the Forest. With the rights and customs of Minstead Manor being so similar to those of the Forest that surround it, and the necessary obedience of forest laws in former times, Minstead is in many ways the epitome of a forest village.

1655 MANORIAL SURVEY

Apart from the court books described above the major source of land holding information is a written survey of Richard Compton's lands made in 1655 by Jonathan Godfrey.[26] This presents a snapshot not only of Minstead but also Compton's other holdings in Hampshire and on its borders.[27]

It is interesting to speculate on the reason for the survey. He is shown by the Manorial court records to be in possession of his lands during April 1652 following the difficulties of inheritance whilst his father's lands were sequestrated. It may be that a valuation was required in order that he could borrow to pay off the fines involved in obtaining possession. He may have had it in mind to sell off one of the less profitable manors or it could just be a new owner taking stock of his assets. He did indeed sell one of his local estates but that wasn't until much later, 1679, when the manor of Plaitford went to Sir Stephen Fox, Statesman and friend of Charles II, whose other local interests included acting as Keeper of the Decoy Pond near Beaulieu.

The 1655 survey lists 54 holdings in Minstead showing their total acreage, the usage of the land and the rent payable. The total area is just over 247 acres giving an average size of 4 acres 2 roods and 12 perch. In addition the Lord of the Manor held 7 acres 2 roods 34 perch of coppices. In fact the six largest tenants held slightly more than half of the land thus leaving the remaining 48 occupants with an average of 2½ acres each. An amount that would seem far too small to survive on without other support. That support came from the common rights that were attached to many properties allowing the occupants to graze their stock upon the common of the manor, and by the custom of vicinage, the Forest as well.

The 1655 holdings are split between thirty two copyholders, thirteen lease holders, six held at liberty, one at will and two by widowhood. Three of the copyholders hold land in the right of their wives, perhaps indicating that the land was passed to those wives by their parents presumably there being no surviving male heirs. The principle of primogeniture appeared to be the basis for passing property from one generation to the next. One copyholder of a homestead, Phillip Stride, also had leasehold property shown separately. The lord of the manor obtained his real income not so much from the rent but from the fines or amercements that were paid on the change of tenancy. A fine or 'heriot' of the 'best beast' was exacted on the death of a tenant.[28] The court rolls for the years 1652-6 give an indication of the changes of occupancy and the funds raised during that period. Fines on entry, that is adding a life, although often around £5 did vary with the size of property in question. The largest recorded was £80, paid to ensure that the major holdings of John and Katherine Call would stay in the next generation of the family.[29] An amount not far short of this, £75, was paid eighteen months later in October 1654 for a transfer of 12 acres of land that had been in the Ventom family to Richard and Anne Cull and their son William.[30]

The fines obtained in each of the five years for which we have court rolls were:

1652	£6 6s 8d
1653	£93
1654	£89
1655	£12 10s
1656	Nil

An annual value is assigned to each holding which relates in part to size and part to the value of the cottage if any. Anne Brookes held a small (20 perch) meadow without any accommodation, one of only five, which was worth 5s a year. The valuation must have been based on the expected number of fines over a period, her actual rent was 6d a year.

Turnover of tenants during the mid 1650's was not particularly fast; five years is not enough to provide reliable information but it is an indicator. Fifteen manorial properties changed hands in Minstead; of these four were from the hands of the lord, six were clearly within families usually by a surrender and addition of a life. Of the remaining four, two or three may also be family connections. One such is first shown on the death of John Ventom whose tenement and twelve acres of land passes to his wife Anne in March 1654. She in turn passes it on to Richard Cull and his wife Anne and their son William at the following court in October; the 1655 survey notes that it is in the right of his wife. It is noted that John Ventom held by copy of court roll dated 8th October 1592 thus affording tantalising glimpses of records that have been lost. The remaining one was granting the reversion of a cottage after the death or surrender of Robert Hobbs, the occupier and his wife to Robert Henbest and his wife Amy. For this privilege Henbest paid £25 for a property that had an annual rent of £1. It may not have been a good bargain for Henbest, Hobbs was still alive in 1674 at the time of the hearth tax collection and it may have been him rather than another of the same name who gave evidence before a commission in 1677.[31] A similar pattern emerges for the court rolls between 1690 and 1706 where two or three properties change hands every year, though in many cases it is the same few fields that occur again and again.[32]

In both instances it is a much smaller turnover than at Bramshaw where during the 1650's 18 of 22 tenants took out leases in a nine year period.[33]

ENCROACHMENTS and LEASE HOLDS

Thomas Hedgis had inclosed 50 perches of land from the common, which he used for pasture, he paid no rent and was only there at the will of the Lord of the Manor. Six others, Roberte Whitehorne, Thomas Mearsham, Thomas Woolfe, Maudlin Michaell, John Burgis and William Ozmand had erected cottages on the waste of the manor and these were held at liberty. Although these might be considered precarious holdings, with little land (most were half an acre or less) and were dependent on the goodwill of the manorial tenants, they appear to be well established. The names indicate that they were of local families, presumably other than eldest sons. Many of the names that appear in this survey also occur in the forest swainmote court of 1635 charged with enclosing land and building a cottage on it, so could be quite old encroachments indicating general acceptance.[34]

However fresh encroachments, particularly by an outsider, were not always so secure or welcome. The October 1653 Court decreed that a cottage built on the Manor common by Arthur Belfry was to the 'p[re]judice burden and trouble of the inhabitantes...' and that he should remove it within ten weeks or otherwise 'the said Cottage shall be pulled downe, and taken quite away.'[35] Some who held property on the common tried to extend it from time to time though not always successfully. Robert Whitehorn was ordered to 'take away and levell the Fence' and lay open four luggs (about 120 square yards). This record also serves to indicate the usual nature of enclosure by means of a bank and ditch.[36] He cannot always have been unsuccessful for in 1635 the property was recorded as half an acre whereas by 1655 it was nearly two acres.[37]

It is possible that some of the lease holders started out in the same way, enclosing land from the common, building a cottage and then enclosing a little more as time went on. Others followed a different pattern: two of which are clearly set out in the court rolls. Drew Penton was allotted land at Malwood on which to construct a windmill, similarly Henry Curtis was provided with land at Clay Hayse. Although Penton is not a Minstead name, he had lived at Canterton prior to his move to Malwood. It is feasible that he may have learnt his skills through work on the water mill at Canterton. His kinsman Edward lived there in the 1670's and 70's; the family name was extant in Bramshaw. Curtis, though again not a Minstead name, was living in the area by 1641.[38] Both had particular skills needed in the parish; Drew Penton's talents were evidently known, for the construction of a windmill is no small task. Curtis had administrative and practical skills; apart from being employed by the lord of the manor as bailiff, he assisted in maintenance of the church.

COMMON RIGHTS

The right of common of pasture in the main went with copyholds, though not all of them. Of the fifteen properties that had common rights specified in the manorial survey twelve were copyholders, two were held by widowhood (a type of copyhold) and only one, that of Robert Lamb, was a leasehold. Those copyholders possessing common rights held by far the largest properties totalling 186 acres 39 roods with an average of just over 12 acres.

There is however an anomaly here. In the claims made by Henry Compton in 1635 and his son Richard in 1670 common of pasture is claimed 'for himself, and the heirs and tenants of the said manor...on account of vicinage'.[39] It follows that if all his tenants are to have pasture rights on the Forest that they must initially depasture their animals on the waste of the manor and so have rights over it. This is confirmed by the Register of Claims published in 1858 which shows a similar successful claim on behalf of the tenants.

There is a further anomaly in the claims of Richard Compton to rights over the Forest in 1670. He refers to his manor of Minstead and of '100 acres of land there inclosed...'. This bears no obvious relationship with any other calculated figures. The answer may lie in the earlier history of Minstead Manor when it was termed a Serjeanty. Around 1300 the land was held by William de Minsted and Walter de Budesthorne, it then consisted of 200 acres and 17s 4d a year was due as well as a service by Serjeanty and the co-holders owed suit of court. The holding was later re-united but it appears that the 'nominal' figure of 100 acres may have originated from one of the co-holders and remained in a claim that was passed down from generation to generation. That this was the same holding is clear from later rents lists when the same sum, 17s 4d, is shown as due from Lord of the Manor, Henry Compton Esq, in 1770.[40]

LAND HOLDINGS OUTSIDE MINSTEAD MANOR
SOCAGE

Although land was held apart from the manor it was often mentioned in the court rolls. An unusual method of landholding is shown in the Court of April 1653 where Thomas Friend, deceased, was described as having 'held in free socage'. This was a form of land tenure, dating back to the 10th century which was virtually obsolete even then and in fact abolished in 1660. Originally a tenure without military service, the services that were required had become worthless. A margin note indicated that it was regarded as free hold with a relief due to the Lord of the Manor. It appears to be rare in the New Forest though received some recognition from mention in *The White Company* by Sir Arthur Conan Doyle - quite possibly this was his source.[41]

FREE HOLDERS

An oddity to modern minds was the system whereby a freeholder could be due to pay a fine or 'relief' to the Lord of the Manor on a sale of property. Alienation of a freehold was recorded on three occasions, on two of these a fine was due 'for a relief', though in only one case was the amount specified and paid. The details of one recorded in both the Court Baron and the Court of Common Bench do not entirely agree. In the former William Olding is shown as the purchaser from Roger Collins of a tenement and seven acres of land whereas the latter refers to the messuage and '...garden one orchard foure acres of land three acres of meadow six acres of pasture...'. £60 was the sum paid for this holding in 1655 which also included common of pasture and estovers. The relief paid to the lord of the manor was £8.[42]   A reminder of the obligation to attend manorial courts is also shown in the conveyance of a parcel of land called 'Sturgions' from John and Elizabeth Fulford to Thomas Browne in that 'suite of Court' is mentioned in the court record.[43] This is the same Thomas Browne whose gift to the parish is shown on a panel on the balcony in the church. Although freeholders appeared in force in the initial court of Richard Compton in 1652, only a few bothered to send a representative in the next three years. It would seem that a request for their attendance was put out, for in the October court of 1656 nine appeared and the remainder sent deputies.

The freeholders were much more fluid than the manorial tenants. In 1635 Robert Morris, John Chater, Melior Lovell, Richard Goddard, Francis Rainger, John Crowcher and John Roberts are listed as such.[44] Thirty five years later the freeholders are Phillip Dore, William Olding, John Purcase, Robert Cull, Samuel

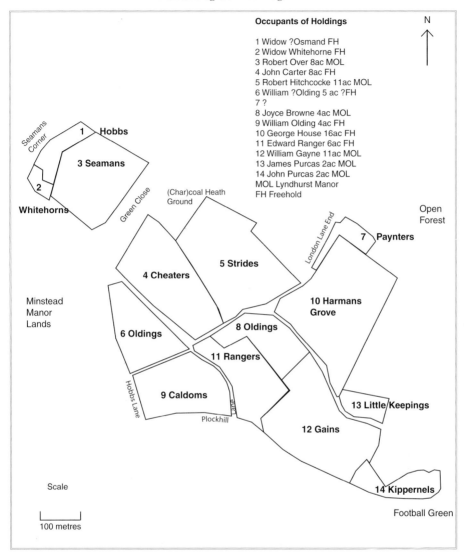

Occupants of Holdings

1 Widow ?Osmand FH
2 Widow Whitehorne FH
3 Robert Over 8ac MOL
4 John Carter 8ac FH
5 Robert Hitchcocke 11ac MOL
6 William ?Olding 5 ac ?FH
7 ?
8 Joyce Browne 4ac MOL
9 William Olding 4ac FH
10 George House 16ac FH
11 Edward Ranger 6ac FH
12 William Gayne 11ac MOL
13 James Purcas 2ac MOL
14 John Purcas 2ac MOL
MOL Lyndhurst Manor
FH Freehold

Fig 9 **Suggested London Minstead landholdings in 1670**
Source:-
Lyndhurst Manor Court Rolls and New Forest Fuel Rights are main
sources, see appendix 4 for details
Notes
This represents the author's researches so far; it is intended as a guide
Other properties exist at this date but details have not been ascertained

Percival, Edward Bright, Edward Ranger, George Howse and John Carter.[45] The last named is usually referred to as Chater or occasionally Cheater. The holding, a messuage and 8 acres in London Minstead, is clearly the same as referred to in 1670. Held by his son it appears to be one of only two freeholds, Rangers is the other, which remains in the same family.

LYNDHURST MANOR

A further six land occupiers at London Minstead are copyholders of Lyndhurst Manor. In 1670 these were Joyce Browne, Robert Over, Robert Hitchcocke, William Gayne, James Purcas and John Purcas; each held a cottage and between 2 and 11 acres giving a total of 38 acres.[46] Even here, on a Crown Manor holding, it is not easy to trace the descent of land with any certainty. A survey of 1787 shows nine separate holdings in eight different hands, the total having grown to 49 acres.[47] Thirty two years later there are still nine holdings though the total was then 51 acres.[48]

LYNDHURST MANOR ADMINISTRATION

A similar administration system to that of Minstead was in place for Lyndhurst Manor. Two court days were to be held every year at which not only was the whole township of Lyndhurst (as in Minstead whether tenants or not) to appear but also, amongst others the 'Kings Tenants of Minsted'. All of the freeholders of the Forest were to attend too.[49]

The origination of the name London Minstead is unclear but may have arisen in a similar way to Bartley with a part being held by the owners of Bisterne Manor and a part by the Crown. In Bartley's case there emerged the names Bisterne (being the chief residence of its owners) Bartley and Bartley Regis. London Minstead being the part of Minstead originally held by the Crown as part of its Lyndhurst Manor to distinguish it from the part held by the owners of Bisterne Manor. A return of forest encroachments made between 1216 and 1244 shows two properties totalling just under three acres at Minstead and may well be the foundation of the crown holding there.[50] The Bisterne and Minstead holdings together with one at Hanger (now West Totton) are linked in ownership no later than the time of Domesday.[51]

LANDHOLDING CONCLUSIONS

The holding of land under one system did not preclude occupation under another. William Gayne who held 11 acres from Lyndhurst Manor also retained just over 5 acres of pasture and arable lands by copy from Minstead Manor. William Olding had four messuages and twenty five acres of land by 1670 which included an eleven acre homestead within Minstead Manor and the remainder privately held. Phillip Stride held land by both copy and lease from the manor in 1655. Although superficially copyhold land may have seemed the least secure, in practice the assurance of tenure as seen with land and cottages passing between generations, actually offered greater continuity of family possession than freeholds. Because the rents had been frozen in earlier times and the landlords income came from heriots and fines based upon events outside the latter's control the tenant of a beneficent landlord was in a sound economic position. Thus the more adventurous were enabled to lease or purchase other lands.

Notes

1 HRO 12M60/64 Survey 1655; *Claims*, 1670, op. cit.
2 HRO Minstead Manor 23M54/2, Book Court Leet and Court Baron Minstead and Brook 6 Apr 1652 to 16 Oct 1656
3 PRO LRRO 5/39, Taverner's Survey; PRO E 178/3097 m 32, 'Foales Gate' 1615
4 Statute 31 Eliz. 1, c. 7
5 1875 Report from the Select Committee on New Forest, No 341, 16th July 1875, Q3357
6 *CB*, 14th Apr 1653
7 Rupert Kepple, *History of the Compton Family*, 1928 (ammended by Little) p. 38
8 *Wiltshire Record Society, Vol 15*, 1960, 497, 1620
9 By 1662 Sambrooke was holding the position of deputy clerk of the peace at Salisbury. He must have been efficient for he was effectively clerk of the peace as the incumbent, Seymour Bowman, regarded the job as a sinecure. Wiltshire Record Society Vol 11, 1955, p. ix & xlv
10 *CB* Oct 1654; Stagg, 1983, op. cit., 793, 852, 930, 985, 1056, 1118; B D Henning op. cit., Vol II, 1983, p. 402
11 Stagg, 1983, op. cit., 440, 818, 877, 955, 1010, 1081, 1143, 1200, 1246, 1302, 1364, 1417
12 *CFP* April 1653; HRO 90M71/PW1 Minstead Churchwardens Accounts 1653; see Haywards in Wessex, Diana R. Mackarill in *The Hatcher Review* Vol 5 No. 43 pp. 18-32
13 *CB* Oct 1655
14 N J Hone *The Manor and Manorial Records*, 1906., p. 69
15 *CFP* 3rd Oct 1654; *CFP* 23rd Oct 1655; Stagg, 1983, op. cit., 582
16 *CFP* Mar 1654
17 HRO QX1/3

18 HRO Q4/1 Indictment Book 1646-1660

19 *CFP* Oct 1656

20 *CFP* and *CB* Oct 1654

21 Stagg, 1983, op. cit., 629

22 Vinogradoff, *The Growth of the Manor*, 1904, 3rd Ed 1920, p. 172

23 *CB* Oct 1656

24 *Claims*, 1670, op. cit., 233

25 Pettit, op. cit., p. 156

26 See Appendix VI Minibiog

27 HRO 12M60/64 Survey 1655

28 See example p. 28

29 *CB* Apr 1653

30 *CB* Oct 1654

31 PRO E 176/570 (two people of this name are listed); PRO E 178/6453

32 HRO 23M54/4, Minstead Manor Court Rolls 1691-1739

33 P. Roberts, Moore Close Estate, Bramshaw after the Civil War, *HFC, New Forest Section, Report 34*, 1996, pp. v-vii

34 Stagg, 1983, op. cit., 613, 614, 622, 623, 625, 628, 629

35 *CB* Oct 1653

36 *CB* Oct 1656

37 Stagg, 1983, op. cit., 613; HRO 12M60/64 Survey 1655

38 HRO 1641A110/1-2 John Stride

39 *Claims*, 1670, op. cit., 233

40 D J Stagg, *A Calendar of New Forest Documents 1244-1334*, Hampshire Record Series, Vol III, Winchester, 1979, 387; HRO 149M89/R4/6145, Bedford papers

41 J Richardson, *The Local Historian's Encyclopedia*, 1974, 1986 2nd ed, A457; *History Today Companion to British History*, 1995, Ed J Gardiner & N Wenborn

42 *CB* Oct 1655; PRO CP 25/2/595, 1655 Easter

43 *CB* Oct 1654

44 PRO C 99/41; Stagg, 1983, op. cit., 453

45 *Claims*, 1670, op. cit.

46 *Claims*, 1670, op. cit., 278

47 PRO F 20/48, Abraham and William Driver, Survey of Castle Malwood, 1787

48 PRO F 10/60, Lyndhurst Copyholds 1819-1864

49 Stagg, 1974, op. cit.

50 Stagg, 1979, op. cit., 8

51 J Munby, op. cit., NF9 37, 38, 69-39

4 Farming: Crops and Commoning

MANOR SIZE and FARMING

Much change took place in the size of the worked manor between 1655 and the tithe apportionment of 1842. Enclosure, of the waste, appears to have occurred regularly over the centuries although no records of any formal process have been found.[1] Conditions may have caused accelerated change at particular times. Parish records show that following the Civil War there was great movement of displaced people through the area. The manorial court records of the mid 1650's, and the 1655 survey of Richard Compton's lands, support the view that there was much new enclosure, both legal and illegal around this period. The maps of the New Forest produced by Richardson, King and Driver in 1787, in conjunction with a report on the New Forest, demonstrate that there had been a large number of encroachments around Minstead. The 1801 proceedings of commissioners appointed to inquire into lands deemed encroachments on the New Forest, found some 40 properties worthy of investigation in the area.[2] On examination many proved to be of long standing, often before the time of the oldest reliable memory of the parish. A few were copyholds, suggesting some doubt as to the boundary between the manor and the crown lands. Quite a number though had occurred over anything between seven and sixty years before. A perambulation of the boundary had been made in 1787 by Forest and Manor officials, this was repeated in 1801 when the former line was confirmed.[3]

COMPARISON BETWEEN 1655 and 1842

To obtain a better understanding of conditions and land management in the 17th century it was thought useful to examine the next detailed study of land usage, that produced in 1842 for the commutation of tithes. The tithe apportionment, accompanied by a map, shows ownership and occupation of each field in the parish, together with a note of its use, size and value. Most of the information can be checked against modern maps for accuracy, and for our purposes can be relied on with one or two exceptions. The most striking error occurs at London Minstead where the land belonging to the Manor of Lyndhurst is shown in the ownership of the tenants rather than the Crown. Waste lands within the manor are listed but no ownership is stated; these were in the title of Henry C Compton.

For the purposes of comparison the study that follows is restricted to land inside the manor owned by the Victorian Lord of the Manor, Henry C Compton. It is not possible to be absolutely certain that the total area covered by the Manor in 1842 is the same as that in previous centuries. However, as it is surrounded by the crown lands of the Forest on three sides and the crown held village of Lyndhurst on the fourth, there is a strong degree of certainty that any change would have been recorded. The one change noted is in the lands recently occupied by the SEB at Malwood which originally consisted of partly Forest and partly Minstead Manor lands. Both of these parts were ceded to the occupier around the turn of the 18th century and so perhaps drew the manor boundary south by about two hundred metres. The earlier boundary may be seen on the maps produced in 1787 in connection with the forest survey.

The total enclosed land in the possesion of Henry Combe Compton in 1842 is 1353a 0r 7p. This compares with a figure for 1655 of 254a 3r 9p. A part of the latter total, 7a 2r 34p is shown as coppice with a further 4a 2r 24p as woodland, most in the occupancy of the home or demesne farmer John Caull. Of the remainder 208a 20p were in general farming use, with the balance split between gardens, orchards and dwellings.

The split for 1842 is rather more complicated and is shown below.

Arable	Pasture	Woodland	Domestic	Heath	Water
313 3 31	600 1 14	341 1 5	60 3 38	28 2 11	7 3 28

Fig 10 **Manorial Enclosed Land Usage in 1842 in acres, roods and perches**
Source:-
HRO Tithe Apportionment
Notes
Domestic includes, homesteads, gardens, yards, buildings and orchards.
In addition to the total of 1353a 0r 7p there was 584a 2r 0p described as wastelands or greens making 1937a 2r 12p in the possession of H C Compton, the lord of the manor

It is clear that a great change, both in the amount of land enclosed and its usage, has taken place in the intervening 180 years. Inspection of the figures for lands occupied, as well as owned, by Compton reveal the most marked change. It wasn't until the 1790's that the Compton family took residence in Minstead; they sold the Bisterne estate in 1792 to John Mills.[4] The result was the building or enlarging of a major house together with the imparking of a considerable amount of land attached to it. One hundred and forty acres were classed as pasture lands and described as part of the park in 1842, a further two hundred and five acres of adjoining land were known as the Great Wood (now Manor Wood). The location of these lands in the village and the continuing existence of a number of old cottages within the park, alongside the old road from Lyndhurst with very little land, begs the question of how the process of change took place. No very detailed study of this change has been conducted though it seems reasonable to assume that some tenants may have been required to remove to other parts of the Manor to make way for the park. Certainly much of the inclosure of lands at Stoney Cross, Newtown and Acres Down seems to have taken place in the 18th and 19th centuries. The evidence for this is both visual (inclosure banks, age of property) and documentary, from maps and rate books as well as a manorial rent book.[5] New lands or new grounds are mentioned repeatedly from the 1730's onwards until the tithe commutation but particularly in the second half of the 18th century. A rate list for 1750 has a separate heading for the new ground with twenty individuals named but no indication of where this is.

One of the most marked changes by the 19th century is the amount of land in use for silviculture: 341a 1r 5p in total of which 284a 1r 16p was woodland, 54a 2r 17p plantation and 2a 1r 12p nursery. This is over a quarter of all the enclosed land at the time and more than the total land enclosed for any purposes in 1655, when the comparable figure was just twelve acres. Virtually all of this land was in Compton's keeping, though a few acres at Acres Down were Alder and Osier beds in the hands of tenants.

The situation in respect of the farmed land in 1655 is slightly more complex because although a difference between pasture and meadow is shown (which is not in 1842) some land is classed as a mixture of any two of arable, meadow and pasture. This presumably represents the neccessity of rotation practised at that time. From the figures available minimum and maximum land usage may be seen.

Arable is minimum of 42a 3r 7p maximum of 100a 0r 30p.
Meadow is minimum of 46a 2r 20p maximum of 98a 3r 26p.
Pasture is minimum of 16a 1r 2p maximum of 111a 1r 35p.
For ease of comparison with 1842 it is necessary to combine the pasture/ meadow figures to show a minimum of 107a 3r 30p and a possible maximum of 165a 1r 13p.

The total that is in these three types of usage is 208a 0r 20p.
It is perhaps seen a little more clearly in the bar charts.

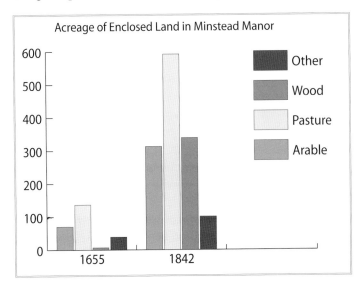

Fig 11 **Graph illustrating increase in enclosed lands and change in usage within Manorial lands**

Sources: 1655 Survey and Tithe Apportionment

Further analysis of the size of holdings provides some interesting information. In 1655 there was 254a 3r 9p of enclosed land split amongst 54 tenants. Of these, six had holdings of over ten acres with a total of 136a 2r 16p, thus an average of over 22 acres each. The remaining tenants, 48 in number had a total of 118a 33p giving an average of just under two and a half acres.

In 1842 there was 543a 1r 24p of enclosed land in 127 holdings of H C Compton. Of these, fourteen are ten acres or more; the total area in these is 309a 3r 6p, so they average just over 20 acres apiece. Removing them from the total leaves 230a 18p for the remainder, or just over two acres per holding.

Both these sets of figures only provide an approximation of the situation for within them is hidden land taken for other than agricultural purposes. External factors are also involved, for some tenants have other lands, either held within Lyndhurst Manor or privately in Minstead or adjoining villages. In 1842 the demesne or manor farm was held by Compton whereas in 1655 a tenant, John Caull, held it. In 1655 it was over 52 acres, more than a fifth of the enclosed land at the time. The average size of holding for the larger farms excluding it would have been less than 17 acres.

So it can be seen that over the hundred and eighty years the larger farms had grown in size by a small amount and in number quite considerably. The small farmers or commoners had more than doubled in number but their holdings were smaller in size reflecting the greater pressure on land in the later period.

INVENTORIES: ORIGIN and CONTENTS

Probate inventories, instigated by Henry VIII in 1529, provide detail of an individuals goods and chattels after death. Appraisals of the goods and their value was made by 'reputable neighbours'.[6] In Minstead they extended from the poor who had only five pounds worth of goods to those with hundreds of pounds. The listings were normally made within a few days of the death and recorded on separate sheets of paper. They are not always complete, sometimes undervalued and do not always add up correctly. They were not always drawn up, and in any case, not all would have survived the centuries. Despite these shortcomings they often provide the only real information as to an individuals standard and way of living. Information contained may include detail of tools of the trade, furniture, cooking utensils, food, personal effects and even some information as to the cottage or hovel itself.

Taken singly they are interesting but their value is greatly increased by examining all those available for a village over a period of time. For the purposes of this work forty eight inventories from 1578 to 1697 were analysed.[7] Additional knowledge has been ascertained by linking them to wills and other records already mentioned.

FARM IMPLEMENTS

Amongst the axes, shovels, forks, bills, wedges, grinding stones and other general paraphernalia of the Minstead commoner are found the more specific items associated with tilling the soil which denoted either a husbandman or yeoman farmer. Items such as a 'dounpot' - dungpot recorded in John Moresh's inventory of 1625 indicate lands to till.[8] The Forest underkeepers were also farmers; Edward Ranger at Bolderwood owned a plough, a pair of harrows and the appropriate harnesses.[9] His successor 50 years later, John Lewyn, had a range of farming equipment including two ploughs, dungpot, drags, harrows and chains apart from fetters and two horse-locks.[10] George Bright the Under-keeper at Malwood Lodge appears to be an exception, for his inventory does not record any implements although he looked after livestock including horses, oxen, sheep, pigs and poultry. Despite being recorded in January, a time when feed would have been short, only hay is shown as foodstuff suggesting that the inventory was incomplete.[11]

In the 48 inventories only 7 mention ploughs. James Phillips had four Oxen but his are the only ones recorded in these lists. His plough called a 'sull' by appraisers, John Stoite, William and John Pococke, is an old west country term for a type that has been described as 'long, heavy and large... It was a swing plough with a beam about seven feet long, nearly parallel to the head and heel of the plough, and with a straight wooden mouldboard, so made as to enter the land obliquely.'[12] Another plough owner, freeholder John Croucher, had six bullocks, whilst the remainder may have used horses as draught animals. Croucher it may be noted was unsuccessful in financial terms for his net worth at his death was less than ten pounds and his son Robert sold the holding four years later. William Gain whose total net worth was £23 1s as listed at his death in 1671 was also a plough owner. Of the remaining four, John Lewyn, under-keeper at Bolderwood, Philip Stride, and William Stride were clearly well off. Edward Ranger, although apparently thriving and in a comfortable position had debts outweighing his possessions.

Hay	Wheat	Corn	Oats	Peas	Rye	Straw	Meal
24	9	8	6	3	2	2	1

Malt	Grass	Beans	Hasel-ettes	Garden herbs	Hops	Fodder	Barley
1	1	1	1	1	1	1	1

Fig 12 **Crops/produce grown in Minstead in 17th Century**
Source:- Minstead Inventories 1578-1697 in Hampshire Record Office see appendix 1 for details.
The figure is the number of inventories in which the produce is mentioned.
There is no clear indication as to the meaning of 'Corn', see text for more information

CROPS

The accompanying table gives an indication of the crops found in the inventories of this period. There appears to be no way of knowing whether 'corn' is wheat, oats or even rye and some of the other terms are unhelpful but it does provide an indication of the form of husbandry during the 17th century. What is not evident from the inventories, perhaps because few were at the appropriate time of year or because commonplace and of low value, was the produce of the orchards. Of 54 holdings shown in the 1655 survey 19 had orchards. Only one inventory, that of George Barton in 1632, refers to grass (perhaps because appraised in June) though exactly half of them reveal a quantity of hay.

Most inventories where crops are mentioned, and this is particularly true of hay, just give it a value, sometimes linking it with other produce. Occasionally an acreage or weight is given such as ten shillings for an acre of rye in 1612 and £1 6s 8d for an acre of hay in 1623.[13] Three acres of wheat is estimated at £1 in 1627 and half an acre of oats is valued at 5s nine years later.[14] Two acres of wheat and rye on the ground is valued at £1 6s 8d in 1641, whilst three bushels of wheat is put at 10s in 1665.[15] A 'poock' of hay is valued at a pound in William Gains inventory in 1671. This, elsewhere in the country, is thought to be a bag smaller than a sack but the evidence of other local inventories suggests that it might be around a ton in weight.[16] Eight years later half a ton of hay is valued at 10s and seven tons of hay is shown at £7 in 1687.[17]

These values are difficult to put in perspective for there is rarely enough information to note any local patterns or even to have a reasonable idea of the yields obtained.[18]

ANIMAL HUSBANDRY - CATTLE

Forty three of the forty eight inventories record cattle. The term cattle is taken here to cover cows, bullocks and oxen. The word 'Kine' is used frequently as the plural of cow. The context of bullocks implies that they were generally kept as draught beasts as in '2 yoke of wooking bullocks'.[19] The origin of the form of the inventory 'the goods and chattels' is nowhere clearer than here where the word 'chattel' is a corruption of cattle implying wealth. Even today (2001) some commoners consider it impertinent to be asked how many animals they have. Only five of the forty three individuals with cattle had fewer than three.

The value of cattle varies between one pound and two pounds ten shillings each with calves as low as five shillings in 1584. Bullocks differed from ten shillings for each of the five owned by Gilbert Canon in 1629 to a pound a piece for those belonging to John Croucher in 1661.[20] The four oxen kept by James Phillips of 'huwine heel' were appraised at eight pounds.[21] Fewer bullocks appear in the inventories after the Civil War though a corresponding increase in horses (for draught purposes) has not been noticed. There is little information to show the variety of animals. One will in 1623 gives colour as a means of identifying animals bequeathed. These included a red steer, a white steer, a black cow, a red cow and a black heifer.[22] Similarly a red bull is mentioned in an inventory of 1629 and a blue cow in 1636.[23]

CATTLE OWNERSHIP

NAME	REFERENCE	OCCUPATION	STOCK			TOTAL
			CATTLE	HORSES	PIGS	
William HOBBES	1584A34/2	Yeoman	37	11	40	£46 4s 8d
Clement PEIRCE	1620A068/2	Husbandman	27	4	0	£50 13s 8d
John STRIDE	1641A110/2	Yeoman/Collier	32	6	10	£140 9s 8d
Philip STRIDE	1665AD099	Yeoman/Collier	21	0	12	£65 12s
James PHILLIPS	1666A068/2	Yeoman	44	10	7+	£207 10s
William STRIDE	1679A139/2	Husbandman/Collier	18	6	11	£166 13s 10d
TOTALS for 6 People			**179**	**37**	**80**	**£677 3s 10s**
AVERAGES*			**29.83**	**7.40**	**16**	**£112 10s 8d**

Fig 13 **Stock numbers for those with more than 15 cattle**
Source:- Minstead Probate Inventories 1578-1697 in the Hampshire Record Office
Notes for figures 13 to 16
The first four digits of the reference is the year of the inventory
Occupations includes status and may be explicit or implicit
See text for comments on individuals' total value
* Stock averages exclude those without any animals

Looking at the list of those with cattle, the number that were held clearly defines their status. John Hobbs, described as a carpenter at his death in 1597, had two cows, two calves and two bullocks. His wealth was not great, less than eleven pounds, clearly he earned his keep from his carpentry but even so there was a need to keep cattle. The larger farmers, of course, had many more cattle. The inventory of William Hobbs in 1584 went into some detail of the ages of them and their value:-

      12 Kine £12
      2 steres £2
      11 bullockes of 3 yeares of age £6 6s 8d
      7 billockes of a yeare old and moore £3 10s
      5 wenelinge calves £1 5s[24]

Hobbs total of 37 cattle was the second highest, James Phillips who died in

1666 had 44, the next highest was in 1641, when John Stride had 32. Not far below the level of ownership of the specialist farmers were the keepers, Ranger and Lewyn with, respectively, 14 and 13 cattle. The averages shown in the table, as with all statistics, can only give an indication of the truth. It is perhaps more useful to look at groups of like individuals to see patterns that are more meaningful. Three of the inventories do not specify cattle numbers so the tables are based on the remaining forty.

The six people with the largest number of cattle all centred their lives around farming, but not to the exclusion of other occupations. Three members of the Stride family were also involved in charcoal making. The lowest inventory value is forty six pounds, the highest two hundred and seven pounds.

NAME	REFERENCE	OCCUPATION	STOCK			TOTAL
			CATTLE	HORSES	PIGS	
Nicholas DONNINGTON	1591B19/2	Husbandman	15	4	0	£33 5s 2d
Stephen TRUSLOR	1592B57/2	Husb'man/Neekeeper	15	0	23	£51 2s 4d
Robert PURQUES	1595AD45	Husbandman	12	0	0	£31 15s 8d
John KIPPIN	1612B52/2	Yeoman	14	2	6	£23 10s 4d
John MORESH	1625A87/2	Husbandman	13	2	0	£50 13s 8d
Edward RANGER	1627AD60	Underkeeper	14	6	15	£44 17s 4d
Gilbert CANON	1629A15/2	Husbandman?	11	3	3	£20 3s 6d
John CROUCHER	1661A027/3	Yeoman	12	2	0	£30 19s 10d
John CHATER	1667A023/2	Carpenter	13	1	5	£90 16s 4d
John LEWYN	1676AD74	Underkeeper	13	8	15	£127 1s 6d
Clement MORRIS	1687B16/2	Husbandman	15	0	17	£79 6s 8d
TOTALS for 11 People			147	28	84	**£583 12s 4d**
AVERAGES*			13.36	3.50	12	**£53 1s 1d**

Fig 14 **Stock numbers for those with 11 to 15 cattle**
Source:- Minstead Probate Inventories 1578-1697 in the Hampshire Record Office
Notes
See Figure 13

In the second group of eleven people, eight are described as, or evidently are, farmers first and foremost. One, John Chater is a carpenter but has other interests including the lease of a mill at North Ashley worth £60. The other two are both underkeepers of Bolderwood, though separated by fifty years. The earlier of the two, Edward Ranger, clearly farmed on a reasonable scale for the area. Apart from fourteen cows, six horses and fifteen pigs he had three acres of wheat making in total over half the value of his inventory. John Lewyn on the other hand with a similar number of animals had all the equipment of a large farm including a brewery and a dairy. His inventory, taken in October, included eleven pounds worth of hay, and wheat 'in the dog kennel' worth one pound ten shillings. The total value of his goods was £127 1s 6d, though only about a third of this was represented by livestock and crops. In this section the remaining eight farmers all had goods and chattels worth between £20 and £50 pounds (one - Clement Morris did have three leases valued at £30 in addition to this).

NAME	REFERENCE	OCCUPATION	STOCK			TOTAL
			CATTLE	HORSES	PIGS	
John HOBBS	1597AD51	Carpenter	6	1	2	£10 16s 4d
Joan CURRINGTON	1599A21A/2	Widow	9	0	3	£30 11s
Richard BARTON	1601A07/2	Carpenter	10	1	1	£42 2s
William PURKES	1603A45/2	Husbandman?	6	2	5	£20 2s 8d
Thomas MALIE	1616B85/2		10	3	3	£28 3s 4d
George BARTON	1632A009/1		6	0	0	£35 1s 6d
James GOLDFINCH	1638AD086	Husbandman	10	1	2	£87 14s 2d
John HOBBS	1641A54/2	Husbandman	6	1	1	£10 8s 2d
Thomas FREND[a]	1653AD11/2	Husbandman	6	2	10	£45 13s 6d
William GAIN	1671AD055	Husbandman	8	0	0	£23 1s
Drew PENTON	1677AD089	Miller	10	0	8	£64 13s 8d
Joan KING	1682AD050	Widow	8	0	0	£36 13s
TOTALS for 12 people			**95**	**11**	**35**	**£435 0s 4d**
AVERAGES*			**7.92**	**1.57**	**3.89**	**£36 5s 0d**

Fig 15 **Stock numbers for those with 6 to 10 cattle**
Source:- Minstead Probate Inventories 1578-1697 in the Hampshire Record Office
Notes
[a] The inventory of Alice Frend 1653A7/2 in identical except for clothing

The third section, those owning between six and ten cattle show a much wider spread of occupation. None of the twelve are described as yeomen though three are husbandmen, as are, perhaps, two or three others whose occupation is not recorded. In addition there are two carpenters, two widows and a miller. The range of values of these inventories is between £10 and £87, though the highest included a debt owed to the deceased of £55. The next largest value was that of miller, Drew Penton, his total included a value of £30 put on the lease of the mill and his house and land. Without these items the spread of value is from £10 to £42.

The last section, those owning from one to five cattle again show a mix of occupations. Only one, John Kinge, is described as a yeoman. His goods were valued at £19 10s but his debts came to £14 10s. The house in which he lived was of some size with seven rooms; the description of goods suggests a farmer who had fallen on hard times. A husbandman is also included in this section along with two widows, a ranger, (forest officer) a carpenter and three charcoal makers. The value of these ranged from the £5 of Kinge to the £155 of John Purkiss, one of the colliers. No occupations were shown for two people, though Jacob Hayes was probably a husbandman for his inventory included a lease worth £30 for a house and land. William Whitcher's occupation can only be guessed at, his house consisted of a kitchen and buttery apart from the main chamber in which were listed the £9 worth of his goods.

NAME	REFERENCE	OCCUPATION	STOCK			TOTAL
			CATTLE	HORSES	PIGS	
John PINHORNE	1578A50/2	Collier	4	2	0	£19 0s 9d
Richard LOVELL	1599A48/2	House Carpenter	5	2	7	£43 10s 4d
Richard BAERLINE	1617AD008	Husbandman	1	0	0	£11 17s 4d
Edward MOULTON	1623A56/1&4	Collier	5	1	0	£8 5s
Edward WILLOUGHBY	1623AD96	Forest Ranger	1	1	0	£8 1s 10d
John KINGE	1627AD37/2	Yeoman	2	1	0	£10 10s
Jacob HAYES	1662AD045	Husbandman	5	0	2	£43 3s
Ann PURCAS	1668A072/2	Widow	4	2	6	£12 1s
William WHITCHER	1679A156	-		1	0	0	£9
John PURCAS	1683AD080	Collier/Husbandman	5	2	7	£155 3s
Ruth CULL	1697A033/2	Widow	1	0	2	£74 16s
TOTALS for 11 People			**34**	**11**	**24**	**£404 8s 3d**
AVERAGES*			**3.09**	**1.57**	**4.80**	**£36 15s 3d**

Fig 16 **Stock numbers for those with 1 to 5 cattle**
Source:- Minstead Probate Inventories 1578-1697 in the Hampshire Record Office
Notes
See Figure 13

Mention must be made of the three others in whose inventories cattle were listed but the number not specified. In two cases the numbers could not have been great. The inventory of Simon Hussey in 1650 although only totalling five pounds twelve shillings included two pounds worth of cows (probably two). Described as a labourer seventeen years earlier, he may have worked for William Waterman of Lyndhurst.[25] Robert Henvest, a weaver, had a little over eleven pounds to his name at his death in 1636, of this the cattle were valued at four pounds.

George Bright was described as a yeoman underforester of Malwood Lodge in 1634, the year of his death. His inventory total of £116 4s 8d reflected the successful combination of these two occupations. His horses, cattle, sheep and pigs were put at thirty five pounds; ten pounds of which was attributed to his cattle and nineteen to his horses.[26]

NO CATTLE?

Of the five people without cattle, only one had any animals at all. Because these are clearly the exceptions it is interesting to look at their individual circumstances.

Philip Stride, who died in 1631 possessed virtually no farming implements nor any animals. His total inventory at £12 16s is low but his belongings indicate he could have afforded cattle. He is referred to as the eldest by the appraisers (55 years old in a depostion of 1615) so may no longer have been able to tend animals, those he had could have been sold or passed on to family members.[27]

Richard Hobbs had no livestock either at his death in 1634. It is evident that he was an active charcoal burner with wood stored in various walks of the Forest. Less than £5 for bedding, clothes and other personal effects was included in the total of £33 6s 11d. Whilst it is often thought that inventories were grossly undervalued there is no excuse in this case as both of the appraisers were fellow charcoal burners.[28] Christopher Stride and his co-evaluator John Purcas also undervalued the total by £3 5s 1d.[29]

John Kinge's possessions in 1639, totalling £48 16s 6d included a mare and eleven pigs of varying sizes. The cottage contained a buttery so the absence of cattle at first sight is something of a mystery.[30] The lack of livestock in the case of Dorothy Rice is much clearer for she appears to have been a guest at Bolderwood Lodge at the time of her death in 1665. She refers to Arthur Oxford, the appointed forester, as her 'cozen'.[31]

The last of those without livestock is Cristian Whicher whose inventory, made in 1695 totalling £15, consisted of hay at £12 10s and goods to the value of £2 10s only. Cristian appears to have fared little better in life than William Whitcher who died in 1679 possessed of £9 which included just one cow and that was taken by the landlord for a heriot.[32]

The above is not meant to emphasize the lack of cattle but rather the reverse, it being exceptional for any householder not to have them. They were very much a part of farming and clearly in some cases were thought of as today with names given them. Joan Currington mentioned three by name in 1599: Primrose, Pache and Cherry as did John Kippyn thirteen years later: Mull, Peart, Gentle and Star.[33]

PIGS

Twenty eight of the thirty four individuals keeping pigs at their death had specific numbers listed, these totalled 241 animals giving an average of over eight and a half for each pig keeper. In the following century this figure had dropped to very nearly half, at four and a half.[34] Pigs have always been important to the smaller farmers and labourers throughout the country but in particular to commoners who had good access to 'waste land' of manors and forests. It is difficult to see the reason for their drop in popularity in the 18th century. Most agricultural writers of the 17th century were well aware of the benefits of pig keeping and enthused over the advantages of the animals wide range of feeding habits and 'excellence of dish.' 'Hampshire Hogs are allowed by all for the best bacon...'; '...he is accounted good in no place but the dish only, yet there he is so lovely and wholesome...'[35] The owners of pigs left roaming the lanes unringed in the 1650's risked a four pence fine and impounding of the animal. Not that pannage was new to Minstead for there are records of payment for pannage rights shown in an extent of the forest as early as 1291 and the woods were used for pigs at the time of the domesday survey.[36]

An old term, sute, now sometimes spelt shoot/shote/shoat appears in an inventory of 1592, evidently meaning piglets. It was still in use locally in the 1850's.[37]

HORSES

The term horses is used here rather than ponies because that is how the animals are described in these records. Nothing has been found to indicate anything of the breed or size of animals kept, though may be implied from their usage. Terms found include: 'colt', 'tegg colt', 'nag', 'mare', 'horse beasts', 'horse' and 'gelding'. In one instance a mare is referred to as in a stable, her worth though at one pound is no more than any other at that time (1639). Values vary from ten shillings for three horses in 1616, to a mare at two pounds twenty two years later; though a mare four colts and a gelding were put at twelve pounds in 1641.[38] A figure of a pound for a mare seems to be close to the average.

With few exceptions horse keeping did not appear to be for other than the individual's own use. In twenty seven of the thirty inventories that mention horses, numbers were given: eighteen had one or two, only five had more than four. Of the latter, two were underforesters so had special need of riding animals. None appear to have been used exclusively for ploughing, they were either ridden or used for carting. Where few horses were kept it was generally a mare or mare and colt. The use to which horses were put is seen sometimes by the description 'cart horse' but more often found by mention of a cart or a pair of wheels or even 'carte horsse harnis'. Nine carts are mentioned directly, they appear to consist of a flat bed with the option of adding boards. One specialist 'Brouse cart' is used by Lewyn, the keeper at Bolderwood for carting foodstuff for the deer. Lewyn's inventory also refers to harnesses and collars for five horses along with two saddles. Pairs of wheels are also listed, usually in conjunction with dung pots. Nowhere is the word wagon used, the implication being that the carts are of the two wheel variety rather than a wagon with four. A harrow is listed in six inventories, nearly always ones in which horses and carts are shown.

Saddles are rarely mentioned apart from Lewyn's, who in addition had another, apparently dress or ceremonial, saddle. His fellow keeper at Castle Malwood, George Bright, had saddles and also 'pantls' - a pad to protect the horse from a heavy load. The word also means a bird snare. John Moresh in 1625 had another saddle, his occupation although not specified appears to be a farmer. A perhaps surprising find is the side saddle in the possession of one of the better off yeoman farmers, John Stride, in 1641. Presumably made for his wife, who predeceased him, or his five daughters; it is not specifically mentioned in his will and so would have been inherited by his eldest son Phillip.[39]

POULTRY

At first glance it seems rather odd that only three inventories specify any hens or chickens. This can only be because they were so universal and of negligible value that they were not thought worth recording. The cock and three hens of Clement Peirce were assessed at 1s 6d in 1620.[40] Eggs were priced at three a penny in 1633, and hens being easy to feed were worth very little.[41] Only one person, Edward Ranger, the Underkeeper at Bolderwood in 1627, kept turkeys, two together were worth 3s 4d. They are much more difficult to look after and may have been retained at the request of the Master Keeper.

SHEEP and GOATS

Six people held sheep and of the five where numbers were mentioned the average kept was just under ten. Clement Peirce's inventory of 1620 contained twelve 'sheepe and lambes' valued at £5 but John Stride who died 21 years later had the most. His '7 Ewes and Lambes and 17 other sheepe' were worth £6;

not a lot when compared with the £40 his 32 cattle were worth. This probably reflects the lack of sheep rights in this part of the Forest; for there is little sense in wasting valuable pasture by keeping livestock that cannot graze the crown lands during at least a part of the year. James Philips had 14 pounds of wool recorded in his inventory made in 1666 together with 2 pairs of shears. Towards the close of the century in 1676, John Lewyn, kept nine goats; these were valued at £3 12s, but no others are recorded during this period. Goats are not commonable animals under forest law so this is not surprising, though it is ironic that the only ones noted were retained by a forest officer.

DOMESTIC ANIMALS

Only one reference to dogs, and that by implication, has been found in the local records of Minstead. John Lewyn kept 'Wheate in the dog kennel' at Bolderwood in 1676. How spacious a building this was is not known but a masterkeeper, Lord John 1st Earl of De La Warr mentions in a letter written 60 years later to a fellow huntsman, the second Duke of Richmond, that there was only limited kennelling at Bolderwood.[42] Although dogs would of course normally have found a place on a farm the position would have been rather different in the forest. Their use was accepted legally but there were restrictions; Manwood writing in the 1590's on forest law:-

> The Lawes of the Forest so greatly regard the necessarie use and service of Dogges, for the safety of mens houses and goods that doe dwell within Forests, that therefore in some sort, some manner of dogges are tollerable to bee kept in Forests... [43]

but:-

> No Mower or Harvest man shall bring any great Mastife with hime to the field, to drive away the Kings Deere, but little dogs to looke to things without the covert[44]

In fact the situation within the Forest was perfectly clear. The Orders and Rules of the New Forest made in 1537 stated that the local villages and townships were to be searched and that '...there be no Greyhounds, Mastiffs, or Great Currs kept no greater but such as may creep through a Stirrop made of a size, the which Stirrop shall remain in the keeping of the riding Foster.' The stirrop, hanging to this day in the Verderers Hall in Lyndhurst, is probably the one referred to. Even so those that wished to keep their dogs unharmed were able to avoid expediting by payment of a 3s fine.[45]

BEE KEEPING

Honey was the universal sweetener and thought to have many benefits: 'It openeth obstructions, cleareth the breast and lights (lungs) from those humours which fall from the head, looseneth the belly, with many other sovereign qualities too many to be reckoned up in a winter's day'. The writer, Thomas Fuller, observed that Hampshire had the best and the worst honey in England 'worst, on the heath', and this in the mid 17th century.[46] Despite this there are many references to bee stalls in Minstead. Of the forty eight inventories examined thirteen include bee stalls. Nine of these occur in the first twenty four inventories, those up until 1634. In the majority of cases the value or number is relatively small but in two instances it is a large part of the wealth of the individual. The worth of the bee stalls of Stephen Trussler, in 1592, at £15 compares with £20 for his livestock as part of a total worth of £51 2s 4d. Other inventories for this time reveal a single bee stall is worth 3s to 4s indicating that he had between 75 and 100. The usual method of protecting bee hives in the Forest, by a small enclosure bank and hedge often of around 16 ft. square, has been well described by Heywood Sumner.[47] Few of the records detailing the illegal enclosures in the 1630's are near Minstead and little trace has been found of appropriate earthworks.[48] However it is possible that a different method was used for protection from grazing stock. There is a wood called Truslers Wood (GR SU293093) on the south eastern boundary of Minstead Manor which could have provided the shelter needed. It is adjacent to heathland which would have been greater in extent prior to the planting of Foldsgate Inclosure in 1830. It is possible that a small railed enclosure would have provided the necessary protection and whilst being illegal on the Forest may have been tolerated on the manorial waste. There is mention of the place as 'Joane Trusslers wood' in 1677.[49] A will of 1599 mentions 'Jone Truslor' the daughter of one Rychard Truslor who received a beestall in a will. Jone Curringtone at her death 7 years after Stephen Trussler had thirty four bee stalls valued at £7 5s giving an average worth of 4s 3d. The majority of these she willed to John and Clepatra King.[50] In 1627 at King's death the six remaining in his possession were valued at 3s 4d each, this despite a period of rapid inflation.[51] After that, however although the number of bee keepers declines, the value of each stall rises to 6s by 1687.[52]

Richard Compton, as Lord of the Manor claimed the right to all honey found in his woods at the Forest Eyre of 1670. Something that his successor Henry Compton was aware of in his claims 180 years later.[53] Honey as a product is only noted once in these inventories, and that is in October 1676 where the value is shown to be an incredible £15 4s 2d. This is a part of the possessions of John

Lewyn the underkeeper and must have been collected by him as 'forest dues' for no mention of bee stalls is made. As early as 1291 an extent of the Forest confirmed the Crown's right to honey though no mention of it is made in the orders and rules of the New Forest in 1537. Manwood who wrote in the 1590's states that the Court of Swainmote was to enquire into the taking of honey, wax and swarms of bees in the forest.[54] Terminology changes too, Bee Pots are referred to in 1578 and 1620 but Bee Stalls everywhere else. Other associated place names include Bee Bushes north of Newtown in the 1870's. (SU267111)[55] The manufacture of these pots or stalls, made from straw or wicker is a traditional craft of the Gypsies. In the 17th century they were 'commonly made of straw wreaths bound with bramble or often of wattle, covered... with a plaster made of cow-dung mixed with sand or lime.'[56]

One of the products of honey, mead, is well documented in the Forest as late as 1876 by Rev. H.M. Wilkinson in Phillips's *New Forest Handbook.*[57]

CONCLUSIONS

There is no such thing as a typical 17th century New Forest, or even Minstead commoner but an idea can be gained by looking at patterns of animal husbandry. Over half of the inventories examined showed that the individual kept cows, horses and pigs. Rather than try and produce yet more statistics it is perhaps wiser to look at the groups shown in the earlier tables. Averages of them all produce results whose only value is in comparing them with like statistics elsewhere. Breaking them down into the groups, as here, at least links them to the lives and other occupations of the animals' owners.

One item that might be of more than local interest is the evidence showing that individual non specialist farmers (perhaps labourers elsewhere, but here typically commoners following more than one occupation) had rights of pasture for their animals over the Forest. They were amongst the most vociferous in claiming the losses that would have ensued had wholesale silviculture enclosure occurred in the 19th century.

It is impossible to give accurate figures for even one village from the extant records, nonetheless it would be an interesting exercise to try and relate the numbers of animals found in Minstead with the numbers there may have been in the Forest as a whole.

Notes

1 L E Tavener, *The Common Lands of Hampshire*, N.D. ca 1957 p. 79 states that Minstead was enclosed in 1852, but offers no evidence to support this - there was enclosure at Morestead at that date

2 5th Report, 1789, op. cit.; *Abstract of Claims 1670...* with a Return made by Commissioners, HMSO, 1853, pp 70-76

3 *Claims 1670*, 1853 Return, op. cit., p. 140

4 W. Page (Ed.) *Victoria County History*, Hampshire, Vol IV p. 609.

5 HRO 90M71/PO3-5 Poor rate books; HRO 12M60/64, Quit rents 1765-79

6 Statute 21 Henry VIII, c 5

7 Forty nine were originally examined, two, for husband and wife who died within days, provided virtually identical information - see appendix 1 for list

8 HRO 1625A87/2 John Moresh

9 HRO 1627AD60 Edward Ranger

10 HRO 1676AD74 John Lewyn

11 HRO 1634AD07/1 George Bright

12 HRO 1666A68/2; G.E. Fussell, *The Farmer's Tools*, 1981 ed. p. 65, ill Fig 18 p. 54

13 HRO 1612B52/2 John Kippin; HRO 1623A56/3 Edward Moulton

14 HRO 1627AD60 Edward Ranger; HRO 1636A34/2 Robert Henvest

15 HRO 1641A110/1-2 John Stride; HRO 1665AD99 Philip Stride

16 HRO 1671AD55 William Gain; R Milward, *A Glossary of Household, Farming and Trade Terms from Probate Inventories*, Derbyshire Record Society, 3rd ed. 1986

17 HRO 1679A156 William Whitcher; HRO 1687B16 Clement Mores

18 A general idea of wheat (and some other crop) prices and the severity of the weather throughout this period is known from a work first published by Thomas Baker of Mere, Wiltshire in 1883, J M Stratton and J H Brown, *Agricultural Records A.D. 220-1977*, 1969

19 HRO 1595AD45 Robert Purques

20 HRO 1629A15/2 Gilbert Canon; HRO 1661A27/3 John Croucher

21 HRO 1666A68/2 James Phillips

22 HRO 1623A56/2 Edward Moulton

23 HRO 1629A15/2 Gilbert Canon; HRO 1636A34/1-2 Robert Henvest

24 HRO 1584A34 William Hobbs

25 Stagg, 1983, op. cit., 336, 412

26 HRO 1634AD07/1 George Bright

27 HRO 1631AD94 Phillip Stride

28 J. West, *Village Records*, 1962, 2nd ed. 1982 p. 92

29 HRO 1634B22/1-2 Richard Hobbs

30 HRO 1639A138/2 John Kinge; Stagg, 1983, op. cit., 1679; See Chapter 7

31 HRO 1665A94/2 Dorothy Rice

32 HRO 1695AD79/1-2 Crisan Whicher; HRO 1679A156 William Whitcher

33 HRO 1599A21A/1 Jone Currington; HRO 1612BO52/1 John Kippyn

34 D J Stagg, *New Forest Commoners AD 1792*, New Forest Association 1983

35 T Fuller, *The Worthies of England*, 1662, 1952 ed. p. 201; G Markham, Country Contentments, 1675 p. 94

36 Stagg, 1979, op. cit., 357; Munby, 1982, op. cit., NF9, 37

37 HRO 1592B57/1 Stephen Trussler; Abstract of Claims 1852 as published in the *London Gazette* Dec 1852, 1116 Robert Whitehorn

38 HRO 1616B85/1-2 Thomas Malie; HRO 1638AD086 James Goldfinch; HRO 1641A110/1-2 John Stride

39 HRO 1641A110/1-2 John Stride

40 HRO 1620A68/1-2 Clement Peirce

41 M. E. Seebohm, *The Evolution of the English Farm*, 1927, 2nd ed. reprint 1976, p. 240

42 March, Earl of (Charles Henry Gordon-Lennox) *Records of the Old Charlton Hunt*, Pub Elkin Mathews, Vigo Street 1910, p. 128

43 J Manwood, *A treatise of the Lawes of the Forest*, 1615, Cap 16, 1

44 Manwood, 1615, op. cit.,Cap 16, 3

45 Stagg, 1974, op. cit.

46 Fuller, 1662, op. cit., p. 200

47 H. Sumner, *The Ancient Earthworks of the New Forest*, 1917, p. 128

48 Stagg, 1983, op. cit., 653-707

49 PRO E 178/6453, Inquiry into Wastes and spoiles of the New Forest

50 HRO 1599A21A/2 Jone Curringtone

51 G Davies, *The Early Stuarts*, OUP p. 260

52 HRO 1687B16 Clement Mores

53 Claims, 1670, op. cit., 233; Claims, 1852, op. cit., 1071

54 Stagg, 1979, op. cit., 359; Stagg, 1974, op. cit.; Manwood, 1615, p. 226 para 15

55 OS 6" to 1 mile sheet LXIII surveyed 1869-76 1st ed.

56 Seebohm 1927, op. cit., pp. 242-3; Rose C De Crespigny and H Hutchinson, *The New Forest*, 1899, p. 85

57 Lyndhurst, 1876, p. 101

5 The Home: Shelter and Sustenance

FOOD and DRINK

The main, in fact almost the only, items of food listed in the inventories are bacon, cheese and butter. This is hardly surprising as ninety per cent of them list cattle and over seventy per cent pigs. Ten mention bacon in some form or other whilst half a dozen record cheese and butter, usually together. These figures are clearly on the low side, for amongst the rooms documented are eight dwellings with butteries. It is also obvious from equipment shown in other listings that most of the inhabitants with cows made their own dairy products. Cattle therefore were kept as dairy beasts rather than for their meat value. For the smallholder or labourer there would have been difficulties in salting and storing such a large beast. Had they attempted beef production a major limitation would have been the winter feed available or rather the lack of it. Most cottagers and smallholders simply did not have sufficient back up land to produce the requisite amount of hay and other feed stuffs.

Nowhere is there listed a form of meat that must have provided a temptation to all - the product and reason for forest law - venison. That the numerous offences against the deer recorded in the published 17th century material do not mention an inhabitant of Minstead is remarkable. However analysis shows that a great many of the offenders are people from outside the area using dogs and guns. It seems inconceivable that locals did not take advantage of their position. Folklore records a number of other methods of deer entrapment without recourse to firearms. Also, amongst the offenders against the vert as distinct from the venison, were many of the keepers. It seems highly probable that for much of the time a blind eye was turned on both sides - unless of course the transgressor came from outside the area. The simple reason for this state of affairs was the comparative lack of interest in hunting by the Tudors and Stuarts; their attention was more attuned to economic matters within their estate. The Forest Eyres which should have been held every three years were in fact only recorded three times in the New Forest in the 17th century: 1622, 1634 and 1670.[1] Although swainmote courts were held frequently, offences could only be recorded by the Verderers, it was for the Forest Eyre to act upon this information.

A further food source is likely to have been rabbits; their breeding was extensively reported in the 5th report of 1789 and is known to have been encouraged by the use of warrens in many parts after the Black Death. Furzey Warren,

Bramshaw appears to be the nearest and was extant in 1659.[2] It seems ironic that as I write I can see rabbits nibbling away at the lawns which surround the site of the former Keepers Lodge at Castle Malwood.

Beer or ale was the universal drink in the 17th century alongside milk. Although the equipment shown in Minstead proves the capability of making cheese and butter it is assumed that virtually all drank at least some of their milk. Many of the inventories of the time reveal either a brew house or materials for brewing. That it was so universally available caused difficulties to the authorities, for unlicensed alehouses crop up with monotonous regularity in the quarter session records; over 1200 cases were brought before the magistrates at Winchester in a fifteen year period covering the county.[3] Four in the Minstead area, all run by labourers, were recorded during the midsummer session of 1646. Three of them obtained a certificate whilst in the fourth case the defendant, an inhabitant of Brook, failed to appear and was outlawed.[4] Alehouses were also considered a nuisance under forest law. As late as the 1670's the regarders of the Forest were required to inquire into 'what persons keep alehouses without the license of the lord justice in eyre'.[5] The concern was that those who would frequent such places were more liable to break the laws of the Forest. Pedlars often acted as receivers and would meet and recruit potential poachers in alehouses.[6]

John Lewyn of Bolderwood and John Stride possessed malt-mills enabling them to make their own ale or beer. At the former's lodge in 1676 there was a brew-house complete with '...one malt mill one Furnasse tow Coolers one brewinge Vate tow tubbs...'[7] John Kinge a shoemaker who lived at Forge Garden with his wife Elizabeth until 1639 also had a brew-house, although it appears not to have been in use at that time; he bequeathed it to his brother Richard King.[8] Others did not have (or their inventory did not indicate) a separate room but utilised the kitchen for brewing. Philip Stride owned four firkins as well as six tubs and trendles (either a circular container or possibly a lid) besides a still in 1631.[9] Trendles are frequently referred to, usually in close proximity to a vat or tub and so often in a brew-house or buttery. The basic ingredients have been found scattered around the area at one time or another. Rychard Barton, a carpenter who died in 1601, also owned a hand mill and had malt listed amongst his possessions.[10] Hops have been noted in only one inventory, that of James Goldfinch of London Minstead in 1638, whilst Barley was grown at Cadnam by Rychard Ecton in the middle of the 17th century, but was also found stored in Clement Mores's barn in the winter of 1687.[11]

Fig 17 **One of many Minstead orchards**

Fruit and vegetables are rarely specified in the inventories, probably because of their low value and perishable nature. 'Pease, put downe for formality 6d' in an inventory of 1661 perhaps explaining why.[12] They are also found on two other occasions; there is a solitary mention of beans in 1636.[13] The area, undulating in nature, has numerous south facing sheltered slopes making it suitable for fruit growing. A walk through the lanes today still shows many orchards; earlier ones are commemorated in modern property names such as 'Little Orchard', 'Orchard Gate', 'Pragnells Orchard', 'Hewers Orchard', 'Orchard Cottage', 'Merrie Orchard', 'Appletrees Farm', 'Peartree Cottage/Farm/lane' and 'Cherrywood'. The last four also indicate the variety of fruit grown though there is no reason to think that plum might not be added to the list.[14] It does not come as a surprise to discover that a third of the manor holdings in 1655 had an orchard. Nothing, though, has been found to indicate whether the fruit was used for trade or local consumption. The sheer number of orchards suggests the likelihood of a sale of some of the crop, markets at Southampton or Romsey were within reasonable range. Although cider is never mentioned it would be surprising if a proportion of the crop were not used for this purpose.

THE KITCHEN - PREPARATION and PRESENTATION

Iron was necessary for cooking pots and fire irons of all kinds. At the end of the Tudor period pewter and brass were available for pots and plates for those who could afford them but wood was still the order of the day for many. 'Treen platters' or 'treen vessels' were often listed in the early part of the century but fade out in the 1630's. Wood of course continued to be used for all manner of food containers, it was just more fashionable to have pewter plates. Even if pewter and brass items were not itemised they were usually valued and often quantified signifying their importance. Pewter was used for pots, plates, dishes, candlesticks and salt-cellars. Brass for pots, pans, skillets, dishes, candlesticks, kettles and, in one case, a warming pan. By the middle of the century the universality of both alloys is evident for even the poor labourer who left little more than five pounds worth of goods altogether had fifteen shillings worth of brass and pewter.[15] As for anything finer, only two inhabitants possessed silver. John Stride, a yeoman farmer had a solitary spoon valued at 5s in 1641 whilst Edward Willoughby had two silver spoons in his inventory.[16] A 'brass plume' listed in Edward Ranger's kitchen at Bolderwood in 1627 is mystifying, it may possibly be some mark of his office as an underforester.[17]

Occasionally a phrase such as 'the trene vessell' indicated not wooden items in general but a specific, a trough in which pigs were salted.[18] Only the better off were able to afford the luxury of such a vessel. Robert Purques who died in the winter of 1595 was one who had 'salting trowyes' as did Clement Mores who had a 'siltte' in 1687.[19] Gilbert Canon had 'a great salt' in 1629 whilst both a salt tub and a 'silt' were listed at Bolderwood in 1676.

The term 'silt' was still in local usage in the early part of the 20th century; the method of use has been well described and is unlikely to have changed much over the centuries:-

> We had a 'silt' made of thick elm wood, which would hold two sides of bacon (cottagers who didn't have a silt salted their pig on the pantry floor), and we rubbed salt into them and kept turning them, say, every other night, for as long as the salt was absorbed, a fortnight or more; then we dried them off and hung them up the chimney and we had home-cured bacon which would keep a twelvemonth.[20]

Many of the cooking pots and utensils described make sense when the arrange-ment of the hearth is known. The fire was to provide both warmth to the inhabit-ants of the cottages and heat for cooking. The fireplace was often wide enough to contain seats either side and would be large enough to allow of several differ-ent cooking methods. Some pots called skillets had three legs to support them and would have been placed directly on the fire amongst the ashes. Others such as kettles (an open cooking pot shaped like a kettle drum) might be suspended from a cotterel or crane overhanging the fire or placed upon a trivet (a three footed stand) in the fire. The cotterel could be an elaborate affair allowing quite a degree of movement depending on the state of the fire and the meal to be prepared, or merely a simple bar. Pot hooks were to be found in the chimney, they were usually large enough to support a heavy cooking pot or cauldron. At either side of the fire might be 'fire dogs' which would support the broach or spit and might also be used to rest fire-irons in. Between these would be 'andirons' which were iron bars used to support the burning wood, below this might be some kind of receptacle for ash perhaps a 'ciner'. Bellows were often used to resuscitate a fire from the embers in the morning; in many houses it is likely that the fire did not go out for months. A bread oven would be situated in the side of the hearth and the flue for the smoke would be of a size that would allow bacon to be hung and smoked. Many of the arrangements for cooking did not change appreciably for centuries and were still in use at the beginning of the twentieth century.

Fig 18 **The hearth at Furzey Gardens Cottage gives an idea of the cooking arrangements in a 17th century dwelling**

Occasionally an odd sounding item such as a dripping pan was listed in the inventories, it was placed below meat on a spit to catch the drips.[21] A skimmer worked exactly as its name suggests and was often used in a dairy. Some items have changed their meaning over time, porridge dishes were used for serving pottage - a soup made by stewing vegetables and meat.

BREAD and the WINDMILL

One of the basic foods of life throughout the centuries is bread, and whilst most cottagers would possess ovens in which to bake it and many might grow corn for its preparation, the work of grinding that corn would be laborious without a mill. Although a couple of households did possess querns or hand mills the manor mill would normally have been used to prepare flour. In the year that Richard Compton first held his manorial courts at Minstead the tenants agreed that a windmill should be erected on land 'neere to the Castle of Malwood'. Drew Penton, miller, was charged with building it and allotted four acres of the waste of the manor for his smallholding.[22] The right of a manorial lord to erect a mill and insist on his tenants using it originates no later than the 12th century though no mention in the customs of Minstead Manor of this insistence has been found.[23]

Fig 19 **Bourne Post Mill, Cambridgeshire, likely to have been of a similar type to the one at Minstead. It was moved to face the wind by the tail attached to the steps**

Mills, perhaps alongside watches, were one of the most complex pieces of machinery in the 17th century. Although the first recorded smock-mill was erected in 1650, Minstead's was almost certainly a post-mill.[24] No details of its construction are known nor have any traces of it been found despite its position being so well specified within the manor. However a great deal is known of this type because it was in use from the 13th century and a number of later ones are extant. The accompanying illustration, showing what is believed to be the oldest surviving windmill in Britain at Bourne in Cambridgeshire, gives an indication of the type and construction. It is thought to have been built in 1636.

Fig 20 **The brick piers on which Bourne Mill rests are clearly seen**

Few existing windmills demonstrate the basics of a post mill so well as this example because the base is now usually hidden in a round-house for greater protection or extra storage. Two pairs of brick pillars (of different heights) support cross-trees into which quarter-bars are tenoned and usually strapped to take the outward thrust. At their upper end they are again tenoned into the main-post which extends roughly a third of the way inside the main housing or buck. The main-post does not rest on the cross-trees though it is slotted to fit over them to aid stability, nor are the cross-trees secured to the pillars - the weight alone is sufficient to keep them in position. At the head of the main-post is the pivot about which the whole mill rotates; it is surmounted by a crowntree which supports the weight of the buck through side-girts and corner-posts. It is upon these that the rest of the buck is built. A large beam, often a foot square called the weather-beam, supports the main shaft of the mill with its gearing and braking system which in turn carries the stock and sails. The tail pole, to which the steps are attached, allows the main housing to be swung to face the wind. The bed stone and runner stone are set half way up the mill allowing space for the corn to be hoisted above and the resulting flour to be collected below. Apart from rotating the runner stone, use would be made of the windshaft to move the various sacks about the mill, perhaps through a series of trapdoors from one floor to the next. (Such a system may be seen in operation at the tide mill at Eling).

Fig 21 **The scale of engineering required may be seen at Bembridge Mill. Each of these cogs stands out 15cms**

Virtually all of the mill including the gearing would be wood, much of it oak apart from a roof of thatch and the piers of brick or perhaps stone and the grinding stones. The materials involved are massive and require a deal of ingenuity to prepare and construct even with the aid of ropes, pulleys and willing labour. The main-post alone might weigh 1½ tons and be 30 inches square and 18 feet long. It is a complex piece of machinery requiring precision work to enable the mill to be turned and operated in a variety of conditions without danger of toppling or fire. The latter was an ever present risk due to the necessity of using combustible materials. Whilst moderate winds are the friend of the miller, storms were his enemy. A good braking system and ease of removing sail coverings were of great importance to him.

Miller Pentons' skills as an engineer were used in frequent repairs to the bells and their housing in the Church. It is perhaps surprising that with his skills the value of his tools at his death in 1677 was put at only 3s 4d. The importance of the mill to the community though is reflected in the value attached to his lease which was £30. Along with most other tenants of Minstead Manor he had rights of common of pasture over both the manorial waste and the New Forest. He built up his small herd throughout his life and owned ten cattle by 1677. He also kept the odd breeding sow which was allowed to forage on the Forest during the autumn pannage season. And, as with many small holders in the area, he kept bees which no doubt made use of the heather on the manor waste to collect honey for him. It appears that the appraisers who prepared his inventory, although registering the value of the windmill lease, did not enter the mill; certainly no corn, flour or any items connected with it are recorded. The lack of a will for Penton, or any further documentary evidence of the mill suggests a sudden end which might have come with a fire. However the inventory does mention the windmill in a lease that is valued.[25]

Prior to the windmill it would seem that a water mill was in use for Thomas Freind, a tenant of the manor, held a four acre close called Mill Close from 1619 until his death in 1653. He was described as a husbandman in his will and nothing in his inventory indicates any other occupation.[26]

ACCOMMODATION

Fig 22 Mill Lane Cottage during restoration 2000/1 shows the characteristic timber frame and brick in-fill. The central chimney is also prominent

There survive in the village a number of dwellings that were farmhouses built in the late 16th or 17th century. These were timber framed with brick infill containing two rooms down and two up positioned either side of a large central chimney stack. Yew Tree Cottage in

Lyndhurst Road, Mill Lane Cottage and the Cottage at Furzey Gardens are good examples of this type. The latter, open to the public may be easily seen. It has an outshot under a catslide roof at the rear, which contains a stone sink, it was probably used as a dairy or brewery.

A huge central chimney stack divides the kitchen from the parlour or 'hall'. The entrance is on one side of the stack allowing entry to either room whilst on the opposite side is the timber stair. This usually terminates in a half landing giving access to either bedroom. The slightly larger fireplace in the kitchen would include a bread oven, although the parlour hearth would be little smaller. The basic design was good in providing warmth to all rooms. The cost was the large proportion of floorspace taken by the chimney stack which could contain as many as four flues.

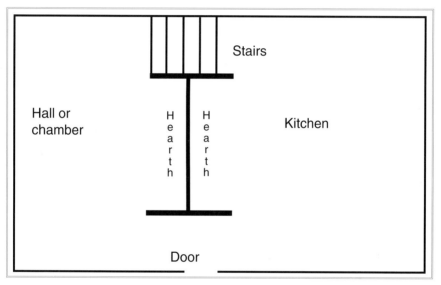

Fig 23 **Ground floor plan of a 17th century farmhouse based on Furzey Cottage showing the large area taken-up by the hearth**

Windows because they allowed in the cold as well as light were kept to a minimum. Some rooms only had one small window. The lights within each window were also tiny because of the limits of glass technology.

Half of the inventories give information on rooms either directly or by implication. Ten refer to a chamber and hall, though it is rarely clear whether this is two separate rooms or a chamber partitioned within a hall. There are also four individuals owning homes with three rooms or sections and a similar number with four. Only six inventories show five or more rooms, these include Bold-erwood Lodge twice. In 1627 the Lodge is relatively simple with six rooms - a kitchen, buttery, hall and three sleeping chambers, one of them over the hall. By 1676 the Lodge consisted of twelve rooms, considerable repairs had been effected the previous year, the amount of timber used (eight tons), suggesting an extension of the premises.[27] It was a two storey building with a cellar and a number of service rooms indicating its use as a place to entertain guests. Despite this, Kenchington's assertion that '[King] Charles was known to have held gay hunting parties at Boldrewood' does not seem to fit the building at the time. It was extensively rebuilt by Henry Slingsby to a size that would have accommodated such parties but this didn't happen until at least a year after the death of Charles.[28] Apart from the kitchen there was a separate larder, pantry and brewhouse with a 'mealehouse'. The reception rooms consisted of a parlour and gallery as well as the hall. A similar pattern of living may be seen from the inventory of George Bright the underkeeper at Castle Malwood who died in 1634. The building is not on such a grand scale but still consists of hall, kitchen, two chambers or ybedrooms and a loft. John King who lived at Forge Garden was another with a large cottage or farmhouse. He had a separate kitchen and hall with bedrooms over each, apart from outhouses containing a buttery and brewhouse.[29]

Fig 24 **An older style barn at Home Farm, Emery Down**

Barns and stables are occasionally recorded, usually in the inventories of the farmers; John King, a cobbler, above mentioned, provides an exception. The court rolls of the manor refer to barns from time to time - usually in connec-tion with repairs being needed. The smaller farmers had no choice but to use their cottages for the storage of farm materials. It must be remembered that where there was only one room it was called the hall and was therefore used for everything from storage to cooking, sleeping, eating and working. Space being at a premium tables were invariably described as 'table board' indicating a top that would be put in position as and when required. Likewise many of the beds were of the 'truckle' type, a low variety that had small wheels and could be stored under a larger one.

Fig 25 **Furzey Gardens Cottage, perhaps the last un-improved one in Minstead**

It would be tedious to list the contents of each and every cottage in Minstead but an example or two will give an indication of the difference in comfort between the better off yeoman and the labourer. It cannot be overstated that the vast majority lived in a one roomed cottage with possibly a section partitioned off as a sleeping chamber. Of seventy three dwellings in Minstead in 1665, sixty three had just one hearth giving an indication of size and necessary simplicity of living.[30] The majority lived in a very elementary way with few possessions. The inventories of those that did have houses or cottages with several rooms and a long list of possessions make for interesting reading but are not typical of the 17th century cottager. Appendix 2 lists four inventories, those of Chater and Hobbs should be read in conjunction with Figure 9 and appendix 4.

Most of the copyholders and labourers had so little in the way of household goods in general that it is not listed, or, dismissed as 'household stuff' with a very low value. Those whose property was considered to be under £5 rarely had it recorded and others have simply not survived. The value placed and the way that some of the items are described or not, indicate the contemporary view of their worth. Edward Moulton's inventory of 1623, taken together with his will of the preceding year, may be regarded as a reasonable example of a surviving record of the early part of the century. The majority of his worth is in his cattle whilst the detail of much of the other household items is lost because it is considered almost valueless.

FURNITURE and DECORATION

It is difficult to give general impressions of furniture used for it varied in quantity and quality between the labourers/poorer commoners and the established farmers. The basics of a chair, a table and a bed often in their simplest forms are all that is seen in the inventories of many.

Few had much in the way of decoration. A simple 'stayned cloth', such as was possessed by Nicholas Donnington in 1591 and Joan Curringtone in 1599, was hung on the wall and helped to prevent draughts as well as please the eye.[32] Their value doesn't appear to have been great, for those owned by Rychard Barton were assessed with two bedsteads at 6s 8d in 1601.[33] Although carpets were sometimes referred to, as in Dorothy Rice's inventory of 1665, they were still generally used as wall hangings at this time.[34] Wainscot doors and locks valued at £4 in the possession of George Bright the underkeeper at Malwood Lodge in 1634 were exceptional and beyond the pocket of the ordinary farmer let alone labourer.[35] Two of the four beds at the Lodge were feather, one, with curtains, valued at £5, indicates how well off the yeoman keepers were compared with even the more successful farmers. Between the better off farmers and their neighbours the differences were of a lesser scale. The number of chests or coffers or the quality of possessions indicating a little more comfort that their prosperity could bring.

Most of the seating arrangements were very simple, either benches, forms, chairs or stools - the better ones 'joined' i.e. made by a carpenter with proper joints. Two inventories mention settles, though the value is unknown for both are listed with other furniture. John Stride a yeoman farmer who died in 1641 had more than one whilst John Lewyn had one at Bolderwood in 1676. They were amongst the richest men recorded in the inventories with Lewyn's goods totalled at £127 whilst those of Stride amounted to £140.[36]

BEDS and BEDDING

A variety of beds both in type and composition were used in Minstead. Ninety two are revealed, spread through thirty seven households; eleven listings failed to mention them at all. Over half of these specify at least one feather bed indicating quite a high level of comfort for many of the inhabitants. Flock beds which consisted of a general stuffing of refuse wool or cloth was the next most common type of mattress filling. The majority of beds at this time would have been of a type that could be easily stacked or stored out of the way during the day for space was at a premium. Despite this standing beds, i.e. those that stood out into a room, were in five of the inventories, all taken between 1623 and 1641. None are shown in either of the Forest Lodges but are, mostly, to be found in the better off farmers dwellings. John Kinge, yeoman, in 1627, had one with a Trundle bed which would have been low enough to be stored beneath the former.[37] Extra comfort was provided at Bolderwood Lodge for John Lewyn who, apart from possessing a feather bed and feather bolster, also had a warming pan. An earlier inhabitant, Dorothy Rice, also had warming spoons.[38] Three of the beds there in Lewyn's time also had curtains and valances - drapes hanging from the bed.

SOFT FURNISHINGS

In twenty inventories no mention is made of any form of soft furnishings though there would in some cases be a catch-all of 'household stuff'. Sheets, in twenty four households, alongside coverlets, rugs and blankets were the most common items to be found. Pillows were only noted in ten of the inventories and cushions in two, those of Edward Willougby in 1623 and John Kinge 16 years later.[39] Of the refinements of life, table clothes and napkins were generally found only in the Lodges and at the larger farms, though only five households boasted napkins. Ten inventories listed table cloths including John Pinhorne's in 1578 and Rychard Barton's, a carpenter, in 1601. The value of each is not easy to see for they were often grouped with other items. The three table cloths and dozen napkins of John Kinge were assessed at 15s in 1627, whereas the three pairs of sheets and two table cloths of Rychard Barton were put at 10s in 1601.[40]

CLOTHES

Clothes were sometimes bequeathed to friends and family, though only exceptionally are they detailed. Joan Currington who made such bequests also bestowed a white coverlet on William Truslor and a russet coverlet on Alice Young.[41] Amongst the possessions of John Lewyn at Bolderwood was found 'one piggs skin dressed halfe a horse skin dressed', perhaps used on ceremonial occasions in his role as groomkeeper.[42]

Although little detail is given of the attire of the period only one inventory fails to mention clothing at all: 'The goods £2 10s'.[43] Five include other items alongside wearing apparel so no separate valuation is available. For the remaining forty two, the average worth is £1 12s 6d, this having risen from £1 8s for the period to 1634 to £1 16s 8d for the latter part. The value ranges from 5s for Rychard Baerline, a husbandman, in 1617 to £5 for George Bright the underforester in 1634 and John Stride a yeoman in 1641. John Lewyn the keeper at Bolderwood may have had greater value attached to his clothing as may Dorothy Rice but in the former case a purse was included and in the latter 'linens' in their assessments, each of £10. Sixteen inventories list the clothing at a round £1. Seven inventories are for women's clothes averaging £1 2s 9d, none being lower than £1 or greater than £1 10s. In two cases womens clothing is shown in addition to men's. The clothes of Mrs Penton, the miller's wife, were valued at 2s 6d more than those of her husband at £2 2s 6d whilst Mrs Whitcher's were 5s less than her spouse's at £1 15s. This serves as a reminder of the legal position. Where a wife predeceases the husband her goods would automatically remain with him, as in this case, no will or inventory would normally be necessary. If she survived him then a will and inventory would usually be required. The inventories of Thomas Freind and Alice his wife who survived him by a few days are identical except as regards clothes. Appraisers listed his at £2, and hers at £1 10s.[44]

The only inventory giving any detail is that of Edward Willoughby in 1623. He had two cloaks, one pair of hose and doublet, one shirt of lockram (a coarse, loosely-woven linen), two handkerchiefs, one dagger and sheath, three falling bands, two pairs of scarves, two pair of stockings and one pair of boots all valued at £2 17s 8d. The falling bands or falling collar was a succession to the ruff of Elizabethan times.[45] The scarves, perhaps worn diagonally across the body, may have been the mark of office that he held. He was a ranger of the Forest by 1609, and a regarder, being mentioned in an inquisition of 1610. [46] His is not a local name though he had twelve acres of land held in five separate closes around 1608.[47] Although his land is listed amongst those called 'concealed lands' it does not appear in the final grants and may have been found to be a part of Lyndhurst Manor lands at London Minstead. Few references to him have been noted; a knight, Antony Willougby, described as a forester in an inquisition of 1533 may have been related.[48] Against this the total of his goods at £8 1s 10d does not suggest a connection with any of the larger families of that name in Wiltshire or elsewhere nor does it imply that any office he held had much value. Rangers were paid only in kind (wood) until 1584 after which they received £4 in lieu of this. Apart from the value of his clothing being such a large proportion (35%) of his total worth, that there should be found in his barn 'one hatt to [2] silver spounes vi old Cushones...' suggests a man fallen on hard times.[49]

Fortunately more information is forthcoming from some of the surviving wills. This in itself is interesting as it implies that the owners thought more of their clothes than their neighbours and friends did. Joan Currington bequeathed to her sister, Dowsabel Ventam, her best gown, one holland kerchief, one partlett (a ruff) and, adding to the picture, her best white apron. She bequeathed to others, family and friends, amongst many items her 'Workedayes petticoat ... old russett gowne ... old hatt'.[50] The latter was a relatively new line for until the late 16th century women had generally worn hoods or bonnets rather than hats.[51] Few other documents add such colour and set the scene so well as this will does in its description of everyday items and through it a picture emerges of her personality.[52] John Moresh bequeathed to his son Robert in 1625 his best jerkin (jacket) and best breeches.[53] Forty years later John Chater a carpenter of London Minstead bestowed a waistcoat, coat and one pair of breeches onto his son-in-law Thomas Simons. The remainder of his clothes went to his son John.[54] Sarah Purcas received the best petticoat from her mother Ann in 1668 whilst her sister Elizabeth had the best waistcoat.[55] A waistcoat at that time was much more akin to a vest and a petticoat has been defined at such a period as a 'skirt ... worn ... externally'.[56]

Notes

1   Stagg, 1983, op. cit., xxvii/xxviii
2   Roberts, 1996, op. cit.
3   J S Furley, *Quarter Sessions Government in Hampshire in the Seventeenth Century*, n.d. Winchester, p. 106
4   HRO QX1/10 p. 14
5   Stagg, 1983, op. cit., 1543 (14); PRO E 178/6453, Inquiry, 1677
6   Furley, n.d. op. cit., p. 77
7   HRO 1676AD74 John Lewyn
8   HRO 1639A138/1 John Kinge
9   HRO 1631AD94 Phillip Stride
10 HRO 1601A7/2 Rychard Barton
11 HRO 1638AD086 James Goldfinch; HRO 1647A16/2 Richard Ecton; HRO 1687B16 Clement Mores
12 HRO 1661A27/3 John Croucher
13 HRO 1597AD51 John Hobbs; HRO 1671AD55 William Gain; HRO 1636A34/2 Robert Henvest
14 Merrie is a local word meaning Cherry
15 HRO 1650AD32 Simon Hussey
16 HRO 1641A110/1-2 John Stride Yeoman; HRO 1623AD96 Edward Willoughby
17 HRO 1627AD60 Edward Ranger; OED
18 HRO 1603A45/2 William Purkes
19 HRO 1595AO45 Robert Purques; HRO 1687B16 Clement Mores
20 Louis Hatch, *Hamptith*, Hamptworth, 1987, p. 38
21 HRO 1666A68/2 James Phillips
22 CB, Oct 1652
23 H.S. Bennett, *Life on the English Manor*, 1150-1400, Cambridge, 1956, p. 130

24 S. Freese, *Windmills & Millwrighting*, Newton Abbot, 1971, p. 4

25 HRO 1677AD69 Drew Penton

26 HRO 1653AD11/1-2 Thomas Friend

27 Cal Treas Books Vol IV, 30 Sept 1675

28 F.E. Kenchington, *The Commoners' New Forest*, 1944, p. 55; *Cal of Treas Books* Vol VIII 3 March 1686; some details of that building are contained in March, Earl of 1910, op. cit., pp. 152-3

29 HRO 1639A138/2 John Kinge

30 Hughes and White, 1991, op. cit.; see Chapter 7

31 HRO 1634AD07/1 George Bright

32 HRO 1591B19/1-2 Nicholas Donnington; HRO 1599A21A/2 Joan Curringtone

33 HRO 1601A7/2 Rychard Barton

34 HRO 1665A94/2 Dorothy Rice

35 HRO 1634AD07/1 George Bright

36 HRO 1641A110/1-2 John Stride; HRO 1676AD74 John Lewyn

37 HRO 1627AD37/2 J Kinge

38 HRO 1665A94/2 Dorothy Rice

39 HRO 1623AD96 Edward Willoughby; HRO 1639A138/2 John Kinge

40 HRO 1627AD37/2 John Kinge; HRO 1601A7/2 Rychard Barton

41 HRO 1599A21A/1 Jone Currington

42 HRO 1676AD74 John Lewyn

43 HRO 1695AD79/1-2 Cristian Whicher

44 HRO 1653AD11/1-2 Thomas Friend; HRO 1653AD11/1-2 Alice Friend

45 James Laver, *A Concise History of Costume*, 1972 ed, p. 100

46 Salisbury (Cecil) Manuscripts - Ref. 132 126, 1609, I am indebted to Richard Reeves for this reference; C Tubbs, *The New Forest: An Ecological History*, Newton Abbott, 1968, p. 149; Stagg, 1983, op. cit., p. 283

47 PRO E 147/6/11, n.d. but early 17th century New Forest particulars of grants

48 PRO C 47/7/4

49 HRO 1623AD96 Edward Willoughby; 'The Willoughby family (of Nottingham-shire) thus had a long tradition of royal service and strong ties with Sherwood Forest' Helen E. Boulton ed. *The Sherwood Forest Book*, Thoroton Society Record Series Vol XXIII, 1965, p. 16 note; Decree 1584, op. cit.; 1620 Accounts of Francis Bennett Deputy Woodward, in Private Hands; S T Bindoff, *The House of Commons 1509-1558*, vol III; *Wiltshire Archaeolgical and Natural History Magazine*, Vol 87, 1994, pp. 116-126

50 Milward, 1986, op. cit.

51 Laver, 1972, op. cit., p. 94

52 HRO 1599A21A/1 Jone Currington

53 HRO 1625A87/1 John Moresh

54 HRO 1667A23/1 John Chater

55 HRO 1668AO72/1-2 Ann Purkiss

56 Laver, 1972, op. cit., p. 116; Oxford English Dictionary

6 Occupations - The Wild Wood

Whilst small scale commoning was practised as a means of obtaining a basic living it was clearly not enough to support a family. Dual occupation was therefore the rule rather than the exception. The larger scale yeoman farmers have been looked at in an earlier chapter. This one will consider the variety of work undertaken within the woods to make ends meet for the majority of villagers.

CHARCOAL MAKING

Charcoal-making, known to be an ancient industry in Hampshire, was probably used in the manufacture of glass and iron since at least Roman times.[1] Charcoal has also been used in the production of bricks and pottery; evidence for the latter in the Forest is given by Heywood Sumner in his book *Excavations In New Forest Roman Pottery Sites*. Two sites, one at Ashley Rails and another at Sloden, show that a variety of hard woods, Alder, Oak, Holly and Ash were used.[2] Charcoal was also used for the production of hot water in boiling mounds in the Forest.[3] The salt works along the coast near Lymington and the Waterside, although primarily relying on evaporation, required a boiling process to produce the end result. Originally powered by charcoal they were obvious targets for conversion to coal when it was shipped from Newcastle.[4] Salt could only be made during the summer months for there needs to be a net loss of moisture to the atmosphere from the sea water in the salt pans.

PRODUCTION

The method of making charcoal in the 20th century has been described elsewhere and appears to tally well with earlier accounts. The author has also witnessed a traditional 'earthburn' (as against metal retorts) at Beaulieu.[5] Surprisingly there is nothing published by the Driver brothers or Charles Vancouver as reporters to the Board of Agriculture in the early part of the 19th Century.[6]

Despite this, other evidence indicates that Minstead was the centre for charcoal making throughout the last 400 years not just in the New Forest but in Hampshire. Over a 300 year period, of thirty one people shown in the index to Hampshire Wills as being either a charcoal burner or collier, (a term in use long before coal was exploited) nine were from Minstead. In fact the dominance of charcoal making as a major industry in Minstead is much greater than this. Twenty colliers have been identified in the village in a period covering little more than a century.[7] This is not to say that they were all solely employed on this one pursuit but that it formed a major part of their income. A few of them were in a position to employ others; John Eldridge was assisted by four 'servants' in 1677.[8] The strength of the trade was an irritation to the Crown over a considerable period, an irritation which was never entirely resolved. An Act of 1558 'forbade the felling of timber to make coals for the smelting of iron', though it should be remembered that timber is distinct from underwood.[9] The Justice Seat held at Lyndhurst in 1670 reported the 'great offence and nuisance to the forest that the making of charcoal wood is permitted for it leads to the destruction of the woods, covert, and herbage.'[10] Twenty eight years later section 5 of the 'Act for the Increase and Preservation of Timber in the New Forest' specifically forbade charcoal burning except where approved by the Verderers, Regarders and Woodward. The local keeper as well as the collier to be subject to a fine if '...any Coal Hearths, or Coal-fires for making Charcoal within the said Forest, to be made (as hath of late been practiced contrary to Law) except in the waste Ground of the said Forest...' The Act also stated that they were not to be allowed within 1000 paces of any inclosure to be made under the Act.[11] Little notice seemed to be taken of this, for in 1789 it was reported that 'Charcoal Hearths are all allowed to be within the Woods ... affording Opportunities of stealing young Trees or Branches with less Probability of Detection'.[12]

Fig 26
Charcoal Makers depicted at Mark Ash during the mid 19th century
Source:- *Illustrated London News* Oct 21st 1848

The reason for the strength of charcoal manufacture in Minstead appears clear. The manor waste lands were outside the direct jurisdiction of the forest authorities, and in times of lax administration the exponents had easy access to large quantities of source material. The 1698 New Forest Act makes clear that charcoal production was a legitimate occupation upon the waste lands of the Forest within certain constraints. The inventories of those involved in the process often list cut wood made up into 'colefires' in various walks of the Forest ready to be 'burnt'. Processed would be a better word for the operation is charcoal making not burning. Regularly used sites were known as coal hearths. Although it was easier (being much lighter) to transport the finished product there was a case for using a proven site for manufacture. New ground needs careful inspection for tunnels and other potential unwanted air corridors. It often requires a little usage for a fresh site to compact and behave as the charcoal maker would wish. One of the fields at London Minstead attached to Suters Cottage is still known as Coal Heath Ground. Less than 150 metres away to the east within the waste lands of the Forest is another (presumably later) site.

Fig 27   **London Minstead, view over the enclosed lands including coal heath and beyond to the open forest marked by the trees**

MINSTEAD COLLIERS

Even if the individual was described as a yeoman or husbandman the evidence of the inventories often tell of another occupation. Many families specialised in the industry, handing on the skills from father to son. John Purkas of London Minstead who died in 1681 was not only a husbandman but also a charcoal maker. His son John and son-in-law followed the same trade very successfully.[13] He wasn't the first recorded Purkas to have such an occupation of course, his namesake of sixty years before was similarly engaged.[14] The Hobbs family had two members occupied likewise at that time whilst a third, Richard Hobbs, clearly followed the same calling.[15] Other families that specialised in this business were the Cobbs with Nicholas and William active in the 1630's and the Strides, practitioners over a much longer period.

Fig 28 **An old Charcoal ring near Furzey Cottage within the Manor**

Some were perhaps over zealous, and appeared before the forest courts for illegally cutting and lopping in the crown woods. Christopher Stride was fined 5s for cutting two cartloads of wood presumably for his occupation of charcoal burner.[16] Most appeared to take care not to offend within Minstead Manor, for only one person, Robert Peckham, was detected taking more wood than he was allotted by the woodward in the manor records that are extant. He was fined 5s for his troubles in the October court baron of 1655. The Strides, John, who died in 1641 and Philip, who died 24 years later, were farmers. The 60 'colefiers' ('so much fire-wood as, when it is burnt, contains a load of Coals' - see Glossary) and 80 'cole-sackes' of John Stride were only a small part in value of his inventory which totalled £140 9s 8d and included £40 worth of cattle. Philip, his eldest son, had 10 colefiers of wood worth £7 as against cattle worth £24. William Stride, clearly a husbandman by the number and value of his livestock nevertheless had more wood and coal sacks included in his inventory than would seem necessary for his own use. His goods were totalled at £70 18s 10d in 1679 but there were also debts, unfortunately unspecified, owed to him of £95 15s. These may well have been, at least in part, for charcoal.[17]

LOCAL USES

The first part of the inventory of Richard Hobbs who died in 1633 is taken up with a list of debts owed by thirteen, mostly local, people.[18] Interspersed with this is mention of 'Colewood at Netly' together with 'wood in Stephen Warricks walke in the forrest' and 'more Colewood in Bolderwood'. The value of his wood and colewood at £13 9s 4d and the debts owed (to him) £16 15s 4d make up virtually 90% of his total worth and this despite being described as a husbandman in his will. Eight of the debts are small, under a pound, and the average is £1 3s 6d. It would seem that charcoal was in everyday use, presumably for cooking as it gives a high, even heat, better than a wood fire. A similar example exists in 1578 where John Pinhorne had 18 'colefyers' listed and there are debts of between 3s 4d and 30s owed him by four local people. John Purkas's inventory of 1682 lists £40 as due to him of 'severall persons'. More than one person possessed a chaffing-dish - a vessel to hold burning charcoal and used for cooking.[19] Even amongst four of the middling size farmers were listed either one or two 'colefires', all valued at a pound or less indicating domestic rather than commercial production.[20]

It is interesting to note that of the four people who were owed money by John Kippin, yeoman, in 1612, three were from families known to be charcoal burners.[21] Another local but steady consumer of charcoal would be the village blacksmith. The occupation is not listed in the records of the time but James Goldfinch described as a husbandman in 1638 had tools that fitted the work. A property called 'Forge Garden' is also recorded in 1639.[22]

IRON PRODUCTION

The iron works of the Weald made great use of charcoal in its production process. Examination of accounts of two ironworks in the 16th century shows a pattern of use and preparation of charcoal. The costs of producing charcoal are relatively small when compared with that of transporting it. In the Sussex example nearly all of the woodlands supplying wood for charcoal are within two miles of the forges.[23] Although charcoal is a friable substance and liable to reduction to dust by great movement, it is less than a quarter of the weight of the original wood and consequently cheaper to transport ready made. There is no evidence of large scale works in the New Forest of this kind. It would seem unlikely that charcoal was carted to Sussex or any great distance to other forges in woodland areas for it would be uneconomic to do so.

Had an idea of Andrew Yarranton, an engineer with many thoughts on improving England's prosperity, been taken up it might have transformed the Forest, for in 1687 he proposed two forges and two furnaces at Ringwood. He had found ironstone in the sea near Christchurch and thought that combined with the fact that '...the King hath such vast quantities of Woods decayed in the New Forest...' he might '...have all his Iron made and Guns cast at very cheap rates.'[24] It is possible that his comments provided the seed for the iron works at Sowley, for ironstone used there was found in the sea and did indeed provide guns for the East India Company, though not until around 1750.[25]

TIN PRODUCTION

Charcoal was used in tin smelting in Cornwall - unlike the Weald there was no great expanse of woodlands - so it had to be bought where available. Yarranton complained of the decay of the timber in the Crown woods 'charcoal is made and shipped to Cornwall and other parts'.[26] This implies that the earlier statute of not using felled Timber for charcoal production was widely disregarded. The pioneering work on the coastal trade by Professor Willan shows the increase in shipping of charcoal from Southampton in the 17th century. Unfortunately few of the relevant port books survive for the town; those that do, show that whilst a small amount of charcoal was shipped to the Channel Isles in the late 1620's, none went to the tin trade until later. However in 1631, 550 sacks were sent to Penzance followed by 1300 the next year. The total in 1633 was 16,100 sacks, more than half of it going to Helston.[27] By 1687 the annual figure was '64,740 sacks of which 87 per cent went to Falmouth'; the remainder was sent to Penzance, London, Weymouth and Exeter.[28]

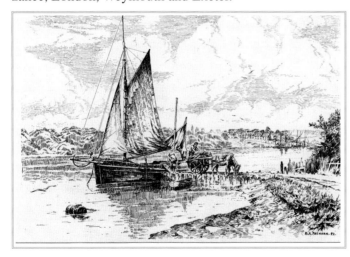

Fig 29 **Loading Charcoal, Beaulieu River by Barry Peckham, 1982. An artists impression of a later use of the river**

As often seems the case with the New Forest there is more to this than just the official figures.

David Lamb in his 1971 thesis says:-

> The coastal port books did not tell the whole story about the movement of charcoal. In 1634 it was alleged that the heavy export of charcoal from

the New Forest had doubled its price in Southampton, leading to great distress of the poor. The charcoal was said to have been shipped from pro-hibited places along the coastline. The customs officials at Southampton were instructed by the Privy Council on 29th November 1634 to prevent the export of charcoal except at authorised places.[29]

Confirmation of the strength of the trade in 1689 is given by a petition to Parlia-ment by Mariners who have 'been employed almost time out of mind in carry-ing charcoal by sea from the New Forest into cornwall for the use of the refiners of tin.'[30] Minstead played its part in this for John Purkas of London Minstead, a charcoal burner who died in 1682, owned a part of a boat. His eighth share was valued at £10; the assessors, Forest men, perhaps lacking in experience in maritime matters, first marked it at twice that amount. In any event a boat of that value must have been a substantial vessel, certainly capable of coastal work to Cornwall. It may well have been the *Anne*, a vessel in which Mathew Woolf, a Lyndhurst yeoman, also had an eighth share, this valued at £20 in 1698. His wife, Mary, was the sister of John Purkas. Woolf possessed property in Minstead, the Duell's Farm 'island', part of Chamberlain's Patent lands men-tioned in 1631, and at the time of his death had a substantial amount of wood and timber as well as fourteen 'loads of coals' indicating his heavy involvement in the charcoal trade.[31] The regarders at the Forest Eyre in 1670 stated that although Beaulieu and Boldre Water were used for exporting charcoal, timber, and wood, the main port was Redbridge.[32]

Although no direct evidence has been found it would seem likely that pewter tableware which is 80% tin would have been on the return trip from Cornwall. Tin is known to have been imported into Southampton during the late 16th century, small quantities were still being recorded in the 1660's. Sea trade with Cornwall had probably been in existence for centuries by then; Hatheburgh Lodge, now identified as Bolderwood, was 'roofed with Purbeck and Cornish slates' during its construction in the 1350's.[34]

COPPICES

Two coppices were shown in the 1655 survey; one used by John Caull, called Four Sisters, 4a 2r 4p, the other by Francis House, 3a 0r 10p. A further acre, described as formerly coppice, was in dispute between Robert Lambe and John Fulford. Many more coppices existed in the Crown lands, though Tubbs in 1968, referring to the early part of the 17th century, states that '...the demand for underwood had slackened...' and '...many markets had been lost to coal'.[35]

This may have been so in general throughout the country but the rent in Hampshire of nearly three times the national average implies there was a demand in the New Forest.[36] The best known example of coppices were the three '...to be felled and disposed of by Winifred Wells...' a mistress of Charles II.[37] The coppice system ended in the Crown Lands with the Act of 1698 when enclosures specifically for the growth of Navy timber were introduced.

COPPICE WORKING

Coppice working was an essential part of the management of woodland for centuries and although it has declined greatly there are few efforts being made to revive it. The coppice system is an excellent example of use of a renewable resource providing all sorts of finished products. When properly worked in rotation, sites can be revisited time after time. It was never an expensive business to operate requiring few tools, many of which could be made by the woodman himself. Edged tools would be made by the village blacksmith, a billhook being the main need. The other essential requirement is the skill born of long experience of country work, something that almost all villagers of the time would have acquired through watching and helping others.

A coppice woodland consists of many different parts, the two main being the standards or overstorey - that is the larger trees allowed to grow and produce timber for the land owner, and the understorey or coppice wood. The aim was to have twelve standards to the acre providing between a third and two thirds canopy cover.[38] In between these would be the understorey, often of hazel, as the regularly renewable crop. The normal season to work the wood was between October and February, hazel cropped in the spring can grow as much as 5 feet by the following autumn. This is important in unenclosed woodlands for whilst there may not be much disturbance from foraging animals during the summer, when the grass is lush, they will search out the woods for food in the autumn. It has other, practical advantages as well, there would be no leaf, the sap is down and there is no disturbance to nesting birds or spring plants.

The preservators returns for 1575 record an example of the system in use. Various portions of land within the north Bailiwick of the Forest appear to be sold off. What is actually happening is that areas of around an acre a piece are being let to a large number of individuals for coppicing at between £3 and £4 an acre. In total forty acres is 'sold' to a total of thirty six locals, Most are familiar names from Minstead, Bramshaw, Cadnam and Bartley.[39] The largest quantity of land was the five acres taken by William Hobbes, the same Hobbes who held adjoining property at Harmansgrove.[40] The land is described as 'clayhill and the hill called hassell hill'.[41] Ten years earlier Hazel Hill had been described as 17 acres 'with a Quillet of wood which lyeth by Purkesgate set with Beeches'. [A quillet is a small plot or narrow strip of land - OED] Clayhill, also set with Beeches but included some Oak, ran to 13 acres.[42] A stroll through the area provides some evidence of its former use, Hazel trees remain on its slopes.

The coppice wood had many traditional uses apart from hurdle making; thatching ties, house walls, baskets, barrel hoops and the framework for bee skeps or hives are amongst them. In the Forest it is also known to have been in use for house repairs, fence stakes and fuel both directly as logs or as charcoal. The skill is in selecting the right piece of wood for the right job. An expert woodman, then as now, would set aside wood for various purposes, only allowing the refuse to go for charcoal making. The major difference of three or more centuries is that the villagers then would be brought up to know their woodlands intimately. They would walk everywhere and automatically gain an understanding of the locality, which fields would grow certain crops and which were of little use. Fields such as 'Starveacre' undoubtedly had a good reason for their name. Knowledge of where certain trees and plants grew and the uses to which they were put would be second nature to the villagers by adulthood. How many now know where mint grows that gave Minstead its name?

It seems highly likely that woodland work of some kind has formed the basis for winter occupation of many in the 17th century. Those peasants and cottagers who were perhaps employed in agricultural labouring in the summer would, once the threshing and other winter occupations had been completed, have been required to help their employer in the woods. Those not so employed would no doubt have access themselves to woodland either officially or otherwise. The lax administration of the crown lands during much of the century allowed ample opportunity for harvesting the Forest with little chance of trouble. There is abundant evidence elsewhere of the corrupt state of local officers during the period.[43] Only when an inquisition into the state of affairs was demanded from afar was there any risk of detection.[44]

Not only were the specialist charcoal makers working the woods, but many of the small holders and farmers were there producing for their own requirements. Charcoal making was only a part of woodland work, in many ways it was there to tidy up the wood that did not have more productive uses. It is sometimes difficult from a modern perspective, where many struggle to identify the species of trees let alone have any idea of the variety of uses to which the wood may be put, to understand the way of life of our forebears in the Forest. The writings of many of those who observed the Forest in later times, including the agricultural reporters and William Gilpin, do not seem to have understood the diversity of occupation of Foresters.[45] The description by Gilpin seems to show a lack of understanding of native woodland craft.[46] This is not to doubt that there would have been those that pursued the deer and wildlife illegally but that would not have been their only interest in the woods. Only one seems to have appreciated the situation '... in the Hampshire forests, Vancouver thought that encroachment of two or three acres meant relative independence...'[47]

WOOD/TIMBER USAGE

Surprisingly only four carpenters have been identified by their wills though the work of others such as Thomas Godden is recorded elsewhere.[48] One of them, Richard Lovell, was a house carpenter and thus had more impact on the village than the others. Although none of his work has been identified there may still be some of his constructions lurking under a sheath of brick somewhere in the village. He and his companions were much more than mere 'chippies', they were, by necessity, architects too. They would plan out the whole building and then either themselves or with the aid of sawyers produce timber of the right size, lay it out and fit it together before dismantling, moving and reassembling it on site. In an area such as the New Forest, where wood alongside clay remained the principle building material, they would have occupied the position that the stone mason established elsewhere and retained it far longer. Only with the introduction and greater usage of bricks in the area in the late 17th century did the value

Fig 30 **Part of 'The Street' of Minstead**

of their work recede. The part that both materials played and their relevant importance over time can still be seen by looking at the cottages in Lyndhurst Road, the 'Street' of the 17th and 18th centuries.

Notes

1   T W Shore, *A History of Hampshire*, 1892, pp. 44-5
2   H Sumner, *Excavations in New Forest Roman Pottery Sites*, 1927, pp. 17, 62
3   A.H. Pasmore and J. Pallister, Boiling Mounds in the New Forest, *Hampshire Field Club Proceedings* Vol XXIV, 1967, pp. 14-19
4   Edward Hughes, *Studies in Administration and Finance 1558-1825*, Manchester, 1934, p. 9
5   A. Pasmore, Surviving Evidence of the New Forest Charcoal Burning Industry in *The Journal of Industrial Archaeology*, Vol 1 No. 1 May 1964 pp. 27-35, reprinted in O'Donald Mays, *The New Forest Book*, Burley, 1989, pp. 317-21; *Encyclopedia Brittanica* 9th Ed Vol V pp. 398-9; J. Nisbet, *The Elements of British Forestry*, 1911, pp. 323-7; P. Roberts, Charcoal Making the traditional way in *Nova Foresta Magazine* Vol 6 No. 3 Autumn 2000 pp. 11-15
6   Driver A & W, *General View of the Agriculture of the County of Hants*, 1794; William Marshall, *The Review and Abstract of the County reports to the Board of Agriculture*, 1818, Vol 5, Kelley Reprint 1968, New York
7   1578-1683; Appendix 3 Occupations
8   PRO E 178/6453, Inquiry, 1677
9   Statute 1 Eliz. cap. 15; VCH, op. cit., v, p. 457
10   Stagg, 1983, op. cit., 1519
11   Statute 9 & 10 Wm 3 c 36, s 5
12   5th Report, 1789, op. cit., p. 21
13   HRO 1681A131 John Purkis; HRO 1683AD080 John Purkas
14   Stagg, 1983, op. cit., 504
15   HRO 1634B22/1-2 Richard Hobbs
16   Stagg, 1983, op. cit., 334, 411
17   HRO 1679A139/1-2 William Stride; A William Stride, agister of the 1660's (Stagg, 1983, op. cit., 1122) was almost certainly a namesake from Lyndhurst
18   HRO 1634B22/1-2 Richard Hobbs
19   HRO 1639A138/2 John Kinge; HRO 1623AD96 Edward Willoughby; OED
20   HRO 1584A34/1-2 Hobbs; HRO 1617AD8 Rychard Baerline; HRO 1625A87/2 John Moresh; HRO 1653AD11/1-2 Thomas Friend
21   HRO 1612B52/2 John Kippin
22   HRO 1638AD086 James Goldfinch; HRO 1639A138/1 John Kinge
23   D W Crossley, *Sidney Ironworks Accounts 1541-1573*, Camden fourth series, vol 15, Royal Historical Society, 1975, Figures 2 & 3
24   VCH, op. cit., v, p. 464 from Andrew Yarranton - *England's Improvement* 1687; The

quarry where ironstone was mined at Hengistbury during the 19th century can still be seen

25 F. Hockey, *Beaulieu King John's Abbey*, Beaulieu, 1976, p. 207

26 VCH, op. cit., v, p. 464 from Andrew Yarranton - *England's Improvement* 1687

27 David Frank Lamb, *The Seaborne Trade of Southampton in the First half of the Seventeenth Century*, University of Southampton MA Thesis, Dec 1971, p. 143

28 T. S. Willan, *The English Coasting Trade 1600-1750*, Manchester University Press, 1938, reprint 1967 p. 70

29 Lamb, 1971, op. cit., pp. 143-4

30 *CSP Dom.* 21 May 1689

31 Stagg, 1983, op. cit., 1671; HRO 1698A125/1-2 Mathew Woolf

32 Stagg, 1983, op. cit., 1556

33 Lamb, 1971, op. cit., quoting Thomas, p. 137; *CSP Dom.* 1666/7 p. 261 quoted in Willan, 1967, op. cit., p. 74

34 H M Colvin, (Ed) *The History of the King's Works*, Vol 2, p. 985; P Roberts, Harborough alias Bolder Lodge, *Hampshire Field Club, Newsletter,* 20, 1993, p. 21; The great quarry at Delabole is known to have been worked for 700 years

35 C.R. Tubbs, *The New Forest: An Ecological History* 1968, Newton Abott p. 150

36 Hammersley, 1957, op. cit., p. 144

37 *CSP Dom.* 1 Apr 1664

38 Statutes 35 H 8 c 17, 1 Eliz 1 c 15

39 See Appendix 5 for listing

40 See Chapter 7

41 PRO E 101/142/15 Preservators Returns, m.3

42 PRO LRRO 5/39A, Taverner's Survey

43 Stagg, 1983, op. cit., x; Statute 9 & 10 Wm 3 c 36 s x-xiii

44 PRO E 178/6453, Inquiry, 1677 was one of many such enquiries

45 Marshall, 1968, op. cit., p. 333

46 W Gilpin, *Remarks on Forest Scenery*, 4th ed 1834, vol II pp. 116-8

47 Charles Vancouver, *General View of the Agriculture of Hampshire*, 1813 quoted in J M Neeson, *Commoners: Common Right, Enclosure and Social Change in England, 1700-1820*, Cambridge, 1993 p. 35

48 HRO 1597AD51 John Hobbs ; HRO 1599A48/2 Richard Lovell; HRO 1601A7/2 Rychard Barton; HRO 1667AO23/1-2 John Chater; HRO 90M71/PW1 Minstead Churchwardens Accounts 1649 and 1656

7 The Social Scene: Change and Continuity

The FALL of CROUCHERS and KINGS

With so few inventories available for any one time period it is only possible to make inferences of change in social and economic position. A case will illustrate the difficulties. John and Cleopatra King were executors of the will of Jone Currington made and executed in 1599. It is evident from this will and the possessions listed in her inventory, that she was a fairly well to do widow from a small land owning family, the Hookers of Winsor.[1] Her husband, Charles Currington, was one of only eight Minstead farmers assessed for tax in 1594.[2] It seems reasonable to think that her friends reflect this background. Certainly John King(e) at his death 28 years later lived in a fair sized farm which consisted of a kitchen, buttery and hall with two sleeping chambers above and 'twoe outroomes'. His inventory total however was only £19 10s and set against this were debts amounting to £14 10s giving a net worth of just £5. This change in fortune may well reflect the difficulties and inflation of the early part of the 17th century. Amongst the debts was one of £6 10s to Henry Goodbody of Moyles Court. Generations of the Goodbodys of Ellingham were bricklayers so the debt may have been in connection with the building or rebuilding of his house 'Forge Garden'.[3] It is of course possible that he had passed his possessions on to his heirs during his lifetime but this was not the general way of things. Confirmation of the situation and a partial economic recovery is shown in the next generation.

The inventory of the John Kinge who died in 1639 reveals a remarkably similar description of property with again a kitchen, buttery, hall and two rooms over them together with a brewhouse and 'backer howse' and a stable. The Kings were one of only four families (out of forty eight) to have listed a 'standing' bed in their ownership. There was one shown in 1627 and two in the 1639 inventory. The will of 1639 indicates that Forge Garden was now held on a lease of which he, John Kinge, had only one half. It also shows his occupation as a shoe maker rather than a yeoman farmer. His economic circumstances were somewhat better than those of the earlier Kinge, in that his inventory totalled £48 16s 6d and the situation was reversed with this figure including debts owed to him of £5 16s 10d, presumably for his work.[4]

INHERITANCE

Although the basic policy was that of primogeniture there is evidence that concern for other members of the family was great. Joseph the younger son of John Stride was bequeathed £40 in his father's will, a considerable sum of money at that period.[5] Joseph's sisters, Priscilla, Mary and Ruth were to receive £25 a piece. Careful arrangements were made to ensure that John's youngest child, Ruth, was well cared for by leaving her the income from his leased property of 7 acres (Water jackes and hodges) until she reached 16. His eldest son Philip was to provide money for her benefit with John's sister-in-law, the widow Mortimer, looking after her. In many wills the eldest son only receives a nominal sum (often a shilling) because he is to be the main beneficiary of property.

DISCORD

An acre of land described in 1655 as formerly coppice was in dispute between Robert Lambe and John Fulford. It was held by Lamb in the right of his wife. The dispute surfaces in 1654 when the churchwardens Andrew Nash and Philip Ansell end up out of pocket to the tune of £2 17s 8d. The sum of £3 2s 6d had been 'laid out' in a suit of law.[6] All had not been well between the Fulfords and the Lambes for some time. The 1653 Michaelmas quarter sessions state that 'Elizabeth Fulford the wife of John Fulford late of Minsteed Husbandman' and Joane, presumably her daughter, were fined for a 'ryot trespass and assault upon Robert lambe and his wife at Minsteed'.[7] Whatever the rights and wrongs of this case there is other evidence in the court rolls indicating what might be termed Lambe's lack of social awareness, at least in the early months of the new court. He was at first warned to clean out a ditch attached to his property and then fined for failing to do so. Similarly he was one of a number of offenders who were fined for cutting or uprooting small trees from the common.[8] Though these may just be signs of the Court re-establishing its authority after the difficulties of the previous turbulent decade.

THE LOCAL ECONOMY

There was quite a wide practice of money lending in Minstead during this period as revealed through the probate inventories. Between 1578 and 1683 debts were listed in nineteen inventories. Some of these mentioned one amount only whilst the most extreme example, that of Richard Hobbs in 1634, discloses he had thirteen debtors with individual amounts varying from 2s to £3 17s. He is described

as a Husbandman in his will but his inventory also describes 'colewood' stocks
in the forest indicating his second occupation of charcoal maker.

The debts owed and owing reveal quite a different picture of the monetary
worth of the inhabitants from that which appears just by totalling their worldly
goods. The value of the inventories alone is really only a poor guide to total
worth. Apart from mention of leases they usually exclude fixed property (land)
though this may be documented in wills.

Where leases are cited they are quite clearly of considerable value and frequently a major part of the possessions of the deceased. The lease of the house,
property and Windmill of Drew Penton at £30 was over 40% of the total (£64
13s 8d). Leaseholds, when they are dependent on lives are in effect a form of
copyhold. A lease was often set up dependent on the 'longest liver' of three
lives. But it was understood by all parties that on one of those lives dying then
the old lease would be surrendered and a fresh one commenced with an additional life added. The landlord would then receive a fine or payment and the
lease would continue with a relatively small annual rent. For practical purposes
there was little difference between this and the older established copyhold ten-
ancies. In both cases the tenant had security of tenure and no doubt felt that the
property 'belonged' to him and treated it accordingly subject to the jurisdiction
of the manorial courts.

Much money lending took place within families but it is also evident that there
were connections to others both within Minstead and adjoining villages. Links
with Ellingham emerge quite strongly both from these debts and also those
who held property in both places. John Kinge mentioned above owed money
to both Henri Goodbodie and Thomas Pullin of Ellingham as well as Richard
Cull and John Stride of Minstead. William Olding of Blashford in Ellingham
Parish who died in 1729 left his estates in Minstead to his son William Olding.
He had presumably inherited them from the William Olding who was active in
Minstead from the 1650's. Ellingham, like Minstead, is a large parish which
includes a substantial part of the Forest and is Minstead's immediate neighbour
to the west.

The amounts involved vary from just a couple of shillings to £95. The form of
some of the debts make it clear that most are payments for services or goods that
have not yet been cleared. Four people, two of whom were gentlemen (indicated
by the title Mr) owed John Kinge the shoemaker sums of between 2s and £3

8s in 1639.[9] Others appear to be straight forward loans whilst a few are in the form of Bonds. Although not within Minstead itself it is interesting to note that Robert Burges of Cadnam had a total for goods around the house of just £7 5s at his death but he is also shown as being owed £117 4s including a loan of £100 (with £3 interest per half year) made to a local gentleman, Mr Paulett.[10]

A duplicate inventory and will for Edward Moulton, who died in 1623, reveals the units of money that people still worked and thought in. The original listed items in groats (4d) and nobles (6s 8d) apart from shillings and pence although the fair copy transcribed this to shillings and pence only. [See appendix 11] That these were the main units that people still thought in is clear right up to the Civil War for many items are valued at 1s 8d (5 groats) or 3s 4d (10 groats) as well as 6s 8d and 13s 4d (a mark). The groat was not issued for circulation after 1662. It did not disappear from peoples' minds though until much later. The inventory of William Gain in 1670 shows a mixture of both the new and old in the amounts used by his appraisers Robert Over, Thomas Soffe, John Gasken and Robert Hiscock. Most though, from then on, used shillings and sixpences as their main units. The shilling was first issued by Henry VII in the early part of the previous century.

THE BLACK ECONOMY

An inquiry into wastes and spoils of the Forest made in 1677 reveals much of this, otherwise hidden, side of life. It also displays social tension not only between the crown and the commoners but also amongst the latter. Many of the depositions concerned the use and abuse of common rights referred to in chapter two.[11]

Robert Hobbs pointed the finger at villagers who abused their rights including William Stride who he stated misused his fuel wood. He went on to accuse Stride of stealing wood from the Forest for the previous seven years and hauling it at night and states that six months earlier he:-

> ...mett the said William Stride about tenn or eleaven a Clocke at night w[i]th his cart and three horses carrying a loade of wood (w[hi]ch was assigned for his liveing in the Forest) to his other liveing out of the Forest and there coaled it up and sold it.

A similar accusation is made by Edith Osmand (Robert Hobbs' sister) of London Minstead:-

And this Depon[en]t saith that William Stride of London Minsteed about
a yeare since coaled up two coale fires of his fuel wood and some that
he had of Pollingtons fuell wood and yt[that] now he hath as much more
ready to be coaled up And this Depon[en]t saith that she was informed
that about a quarter of a yeare since the said Stride cutt downe five trees
in the Castle of Mallwood walke about Hardish greene and Lundon lane
end for fuell and that she saw the said Stride about a quarter of a yeare
since carry home five loads some he coaled up and others he fagotted And
this Depon[en]t further saith that about Mich[aelma]s last he made a very
greate many of pales out of the fuell wood and carried them to his liveing
in Mr Comptons liberty And this Depon[en]t saith that she had seen the
said Stride and his sonne for a week together since Mich[aelma]s carrying
home browse wood w[hi]ch they stole and cutt up into Coale fires.

Robert Hobbs accused William Olding of using unassigned trees from the
Forest for building purposes. Edith Osmand, states that he has built three tenements and a barn, employing two sawyers, John Henvest and Thomas Buckle
for nearly a year. She also mentions that Olding was employed as a carrier of
the king's timber to Redbridge, and used his position to his own advantage,
misappropriating timber on occasion. This may be a reference to timber that
was seized by a Captain Edmond Green in 1670 as belonging to the Crown.
Olding, alongside another witness, Henry Furster, who held the *Blue Anchor* at
Redbridge, claimed that the timber came from Richard Edwards' land at Bramshaw.[12]

Accusations against John Martin indicate more of the burgeoning timber trade.
He is stated to have sold two loads of coopers boards and so much cleft timber
'as five horses could draw to Salisbury or Fordingbridge'. Edith Osmand also
claimed that he kept 'Buckett tymber' at his house made out of wood assigned
him for fuel. Martin was not alone in this market for Thomas Cowdrey, who
bought Harmans Grove at London Minstead in 1665 also followed this occupation.[13] Robert Over, who held Seamans in 1670, apparently worked a three
day week selling wood in Totton and Southampton on Monday, Wednesday and
Friday, a practice he carried out for 16 years. The implication is that the wood
is stolen; the informer, his neighbour Edith Osmand, challenged him with the
result that he grew his hedges higher so that she could not see him leaving his
property by the back way through the forest.

Osmand's brother though appeared to miss no one in his deposition for he even
included William Royal the Minister of the parish. Some of the accusations are
concerned with general removal of timber illegally from the Forest as well as

others taking it under pretence of fuel wood. The list is long, apart from those already named there are Mathew Woolfe, William Purcas, collier, William Wrighte, saddletree maker, Edward Wright, timber feller and Richard Symonds, collier; reading almost like a trade directory of the time.[14]

LITERACY

Few books are mentioned in the wills and inventories of Minstead. Ruth Cull had a great bible which she gave to Richard Cull her grandchild.[15] John Chater of London Minstead, a carpenter, left books (untitled) valued at 3s 4d in his inventory.[16] In fact only Bibles are specified; John Stride left four on his death and two appeared in the inventory of his son Philip twenty four years later in 1665. Their value together with an unknown quantity of other books is £1 6s 8d. It is apparent that not only could many members of the Stride family read but that they could write for they acted as scriveners, preparing wills for their neighbours.

John Gane of Minstead wrote the will of Thomas Malie but John Stride also witnessed and signed it.[17] Seven years later Stride wrote the will of Edward Moulton whilst Christopher Stride was an appraiser who wrote the inventory.[18] An original as well as a fair copy is extant for both of these. John Stride again signed the inventory of John Kinge in which appears a debt to Stride of £1; whether this was for his services for writing the inventory, providing charcoal or some other cause is not known.[19] Ironically his own will was written by Thomas King cleric, presumably because he was too weak to do so.[20]

Others who were able to write included William Stride who signed his own will in 1679.[21] John Call wrote the will of Gilbert Canon in 1629 whilst five years later Richard Gaine witnessed with his own signature the will of Richard Hobbs.[22] William Hele appears as the writer of a number of wills including those of John Kinge and James Goldfinch.[23] Henry Curtis wrote the inventory of John Stride.[24] All of these were either successful farmers or were employed in work in which ability to read and write was a pre-requisite. The question is did they learn to read and write because they (or their families) were successful or was it the other way around?

Marks are used in many wills and are quite recognisable in some cases. Richard Henvest used RH when witnessing his father's will, Thomas Hedges an H and John Purcas I P (I's and J's were interchangeable).[25]

POPULATION

It is possible with modern techniques to establish population and population trends from parish registers; unfortunately these do not exist for Minstead until 1682. The closest we get for an earlier period is the purchase of a register in 1653. Figures may be interpolated from two major sources although it must be remembered that neither was intended to produce a population count. The Compton Census of 1676 (a national census that the Bishop of London administered) includes the following local figures:-

	Eling	Minstead	Lyndhurst
Conformists	650	287	257
Papists	7	9	0
Nonconformists	30	8	6
Total	687	304	263
Population*	1145	506	438

Fig 31 **Population information for 1676**
Source:- A. Whiteman, The Compton Census of 1676, 1986, pp. 89-90
* Estimated figure, see below for method

The census was taken of all adults over 16, if it is assumed that 40% of the population is under that age then the multiplier is 5/3 giving the population shown.

This can be checked against the published Hearth Tax returns for 1665 which lists households. The situation is a little complicated because there are separate figures for Minstead and London Minstead (including Bartley Regis) whilst Canterton is accounted for with Fritham, and Cadnam is partly in Minstead and partly in Eling. 29 households are shown at Minstead as chargeable and 35 households not chargeable giving a total of 64. Taking the generally accepted multiplier of 4½, as being the average occupancy per household, this gives 288 individuals.

Bartley Regis and London Minstead shown as another administrative unit had 24 households chargeable and 15 not chargeable for the Hearth Tax. Hearth Tax collection was based on the parish rates, generally speaking those paying it were liable to pay Hearth Tax. The rates list for this time shows 8 people paying rates at London Minstead. Taking this as a proportion (a third) of the figures above indicates that there were probably 5 households not chargeable. So there was likely to be around 13 households at London Minstead and the remainder, 26, at

Bartley Regis. This would suggest that approximately 55-60 people are living at London Minstead.

The combined figure for Minstead and London Minstead then is likely to be around 340-350 occupants. Inevitably there will have been some dwellings that were missed or overlooked, obvious examples are the two Forest Lodges (both of these appear in a list for 1674 but not 1665).[26] Whilst absolute accuracy cannot be claimed the figures are in line with the Compton Census figures bearing in mind the latter included Canterton and part of Cadnam.

For comparative purposes the following figures for Minstead parish include those taken from the official census returns made mainly in the 19th century.

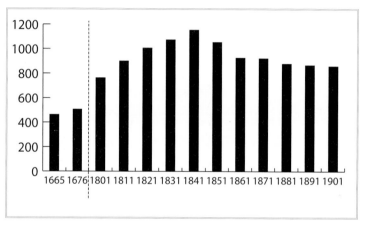

Fig 32 **Minstead population estimates in the 17th century compared to the official census figures for the 19th century**

Sources and notes

See text for 17th C calculation methods

Remaining figures from *Victoria County History Hampshire*, Vol V p. 446

NB The 1665 figures do not include those parts of Canterton and Cadnam within the parish but do include Bartley Regis

WEALTH and POVERTY

The Hearth Tax assessments can also be used to provide a basis for inquiry into relative wealth and poverty. It was paid by occupiers at an annual levy of 2 shillings per hearth, due Michaelmas (29th September) and Lady Day (25th March).[27] Originally exemptions from this tax were granted to people not paying poor rates as well as those whose property was not worth an annual rent of 20 shillings and who did not possess goods or lands to the value of £10. This changed in 1664 to make liable all who had a dwelling with more than two hearths.[28] The 77 dwellings in Minstead include a total of 105 hearths giving an average of less than one and a half (1.36). It is misleading to compare averages with other villages because of distortions created by a small number of large houses with a large number of hearths. A better means of comparison is perhaps the percentage of households in each village that are exempted from the tax.

VILLAGE	HOUSEHOLDS	POPULATION IMPLIED	HEARTHS	% WITH 1 HEARTH	% NOT PAYING TAX
Bisterne & Crow	65	292	115	72	35
Brockenhurst	95	427	186	60	22
Burley	64	288	96	73	31
Canterton & Fritham	73	328	132	63	40
Godshill	59	265	89	81	34
Hythe	34	153	61	56	56
Lyndhurst	71	319	165	59	30
Minstead	77	346	105	82	52

Fig 33 **New Forest Population Figures Based on the 1665 Hearth Tax Returns**
Source:- *The Hampshire Hearth Tax Assessment 1665*, Ed. Elizabeth Hughes and Philippa White, Hampshire Record Series Vol XI, 1991
Notes
The population implied is based on four and half people per household. See text for discussion
The Hythe figure does not include Butts Ash, Dibden or outlying parts

The table gives a comparison for a number of Forest communities. The villages have been chosen to give a wide geographical spread within the Forest; some are better as representative units than others. In each case the figures must be viewed with some caution for there are known omissions and sometimes the inclusion of just one dwelling can make an enormous difference to the statistics. Richard Compton's own Tudor house at Bisterne for example, taxed for 21 hearths and included in Bisterne and Crow, increases the hearths there by over 20%.

What is clear though is that the villages of Burley, Bisterne with Crow and particularly Godshill and Minstead had a greater concentration of the poorer people living in a simple way than any others. The deceptiveness of such figures is shown with Hythe, which, although having a greater number of houses with two or more Hearths, actually has less people (as a percentage) paying tax than any other Forest community.

HARMANSGROVE - LAND LOST and LAND GAINED

The fortunes of two families on the same plot of land provide instances of fortune both good and bad in the 17th century.

In December 1572 William Hobbes, a husbandman of Minstead obtained a close of land called Harmansgrove from Thomas Suttun of Southampton.[29] It lies at the easternmost end of London Minstead, opposite Perry's farm and no doubt was once encroached from the Forest (GR SU285115). It is possible that this land is not unconnected with a 15 acre wood described as mostly oak in 1565 between 'Newlands End and Dagbournes'. [Dogben Gutter][30] By 1584 the land was used for a combination of rough grazing, coppicing and winter feed (hay). On Hobbes' death his wife, Anne, was with their son John, to have the benefit of the grazing and the fuel available on the property. The house at that stage was single storey consisting of a main room or hall with a bedroom or chamber probably partitioned, off and a kitchen. The latter was likely to have been a narrow area not unlike the kitchen to be seen at Furzey Gardens Cottage.

Hobbs grudgingly acknowledged a debt to Thomas Suttun of 13s 4d in his will shortly before he died but clearly there had been no communication between them for some time: '...yf he be alive and do come in his owne person to demand it...' However the value of his inventory at over £46 indicated that he had prospered and indeed his son, a couple of years later, was shown to be one of the most heavily taxed men in the parish.[31] In 1608 Harmansgrove comprised a cottage and 17a 2r 25p of woodland. It featured in a list of purprestures or encroachments that the Crown granted to two Londoners, George Merreil and Thomas Ely. The usual practice was for the grantees to negotiate with the possessors and allow the illegal enclosure to stand for a fee. In many cases the Crown returned at a later date and extorted a further sum from the current occupier.[32] In this instance it is known that a member of the Hobbs family, another William, was in possession in 1608 but that by 1635 the property was occupied by John Croucher, a yeoman freeholder.

At this time the land had been divided into eight closes and developed with the addition of a second cottage together with an orchard and twelve acres of arable land, two acres of meadow and six acres of pasture. Croucher lived in one cottage, the other was let to John Paynter, a labourer. The second cottage had been built by John Paynter who had also enclosed a couple of perches of the 'king's desmesne'. They both fell victim to the efforts of Charles I to raise money by stringent use of forest law in the 1630's. Each had to pay a fine of £3 for erecting the cottage with Paynter forfeiting an additional 20s for the encroachment.[33] Paynter's father, also John, had held property at London Minstead as part of Lyndhurst Manor but this had passed to his daughter, Anna, on his death ten years earlier.[34] The additional fields enclosed at this time are clearly seen on the 19th century maps.

Croucher, a respected member of the community played his part in village affairs. As possessor of a large amount of land he paid a proportionately large rate, and was for some years on the Church Vestry committee which set that rate. However by the time of his death in 1661 serious financial difficulties had beset him. Whether his involvement in the Blake murder case, mentioned below, played a part in his hardships is not known; it is noted that one of the appraisers of his inventory is a Thomas Blake. His goods were valued at a little under £31 pounds whilst his debts totalling almost £22 did not include an undisclosed amount owing to Thomas Browne mentioned in the will. His affairs were clearly in a perilous state for one of the overseers of his will, neighbour John Stantor, made a plea to those assessing his debts to '...take this poore widdows sadd condicon unto yo[u]r favorable consideracon...'[35]

Eldest son, Robert, tried to make a go of it but was forced to sell the property four years later to Thomas Cowdrey a bucket maker. How much of the consideration of £200 stayed with the family is not known. Cowdrey did not keep the estate long for George House and his wife, Mary, were in possession of it by 1669 having paid the same sum. They claimed rights of pasture and pannage the following year over the Forest; by this time the size was given as 16 acres. They also leased an additional 12 acres from Edward Bright.[36] Harmansgrove was retained in their possession and that of their son Moses, a collier, until 1694. Following the sale to Fordingbridge man, John Norris, it was subsequently known as Norris's. One of the smaller creditors of Croucher in 1661 was a William Kent of Romsey, this is thought to be the first interest of that family in Minstead. They played a large part in the farming of not only Norris's but London Minstead during the 18th and 19th century.

TREATMENT of the POOR

At times the workings of the manorial court and that of the parish authorities seems very close. In October 1656 at the Frankpledge Court George House was presented for taking in a lodger, a widow, and threatened with a fine of 20s if he had not evicted her before the following Lady Day. She is described as a 'poore woman' so the concern would seem to be that she might become a drain on the parish rather than the risk of her staking a claim on the property. The churchwardens accounts for 1655 reveal a similar situation whereby John Croucher was bound for 'yeelding houseroome to Grace Stride' no doubt for the same reason.

Separate accounts for the overseers of the poor do not occur until the 1690's, few of the earlier entries, contained in the churchwardens accounts, give much direct information on the inhabitants. One, of 1662, does indicate a problem though not its nature 'goinge the gestes [justices] for a warent for Perryes childrens'. It may well be relevant to a section of the 1601 poor relief Act in which parents and grandparents were liable for maintenance of their children first and foremost rather than the parish. Responsibilities and loyalties to family and friends are occasionally glimpsed. Christpian Kember died young though not too young to have a daughter, Elizabeth. Her father obtained a bond for ten pounds for the maintenance of mother and child from Thomas Burges of Cadnam. On her death bed Christpian delivered her thoughts on that money and her fondness for Thomas and his brother. Eight pounds were to be used for the benefit of Elizabeth and two were to go to her (Christpian's) father. However if her daughter should die before full age then four pounds was to go to Thomas Burges the younger and four pounds to his brother William Burges.[37]

CHURCHWARDENS' ACCOUNTS

The accounts produced by the churchwardens every year indicate some of the social problems of the day and the way in which they were handled. Many of the disbursements are mirrored all over the county at this period for their origin is not in local charity but in Statute such as the Elizabethan Poor Relief Act of 1601.[38] This Act remained the foundation of relief until the 19th century, the basic principle behind it of differentiating between the 'deserving' and the 'undeserving' poor carried on into the early part of the 20th century and has even been revived at its close. It was originally only intended to last until the end of the current session of parliament but was extended before being made permanent in 1640. Changing times of course meant that amendments and additions were necessary, the most important was the Act of 1662 which ensured that anyone new to a parish would not become a burden upon it.[39]

The routine payments included 'gaole and marshall' i.e. payments for food for the poor in gaol; and those who suffer loss at sea or through fire and visitation - the regular visit to present the state of affairs in the parish to the Bishop.[40] Payments for bread and wine 'Pinte of Sacke' used during the service and washing the church linen were commonplace as were fees paid to bell ringers and for fox heads. Regular amounts were needed for travellers and quite often for mending the bells. Small repairs would be undertaken by the clerk, Henry Curtis, but often it required more technical work in which Drew Penton was called to assist him. Large numbers of seamen travelled through the parish and received some form of help. Many that were paid had a 'Pass' indicating that they were not to be treated as vagrants. One such, who received 6d from the parish in 1641, was described as having been 'taken by the Dunkecks', this presumably is a reference to pirates who still operated out of Dunkirk. They had caused losses to English trade for decades and continued to do so until 1658.[41] A payment of 2s is recorded by Thomas Frend, Churchwarden, in 1641 for a new paper book, presumably the one recording its purchase. Apprentices were covered by the Poor Relief Act of 1601 but only one entry, for 1658, has been found when one of the wardens visited Ringwood. An entry in Fordingbridge records for 1671 indicates that John Stride, a tailor of Minstead, took on an apprentice, Giles Ashe.[42] Another parishioner from the Avon valley, Ambrose Ringwood of Nether Burgate, is mentioned in connection with supporting Thomas, the bastard child of Jane Newman.[43] These isolated cases, found in neighbouring parish records, touching on Minstead residents perhaps indicate the nature of events which would have occurred in Minstead.

There was a need for a certain amount of travel by the churchwardens. Although, unlike the overseers of the poor, they were not required to be 'substantial householders' in practice they do, at this period, appear to be men of some import and so would probably have had their own transport. Official journeys during the period 1641-70 covered Lyndhurst, Lymington, Totton, Ringwood, Redlynch, Toothill, Winchester, Southampton, Brockenhurst and Romsey. Totton was only shown the once, 1641, in connection with the protestation oaths that parliament organised against the possibility of 'an arbitrary and tyrannical government'.[44] Andrew Nash's horse ride to Southampton in 1653, which visit was the only one in this period, cost the parish two shillings. The purpose was to purchase a register, probably in connection with an ordinance of the Barebone's Parliament to allow civil marriage.[45] Sadly that register is not known to have survived the years. Most of the journeys to Winchester were for the visitations required by the Bishop, which enabled him to inquire into the spiritual health of the community and the efficiency of his minister. An exception was the trip of Robert Soaf in 1659 about first fruits, originally a papal taxation of the clergy but appropriated by Henry VIII. It was the first years salary of a newly appointed member of the clergy.[46]

Visits to Lyndhurst were usually in connection with the Court held there. The amounts claimed by different or even in some cases the same churchwarden for the same journey varied. Expenses for excursions to Ringwood fluctuated between one shilling, one shilling and eight pence and two shillings. Wine for the sacrament was obtained from Romsey.

There are many reminders of the troubles both in England and elsewhere with many strangers passing through the parish. Two women from Ireland were assisted in 1641 'their husbands being slaine'. The fighting in Ireland showed up with an entry for October 29th 1649 whereby '14 Irish [applied] for relief from the Parliament.' The following year a total of twenty nine Irish people received relief. A further sixteen were helped in 1651 along with eight 'Maymed Soldirs'. These problems did not abate in subsequent years although the detail recorded varies with the churchwarden. In 1653 there were more payments to maimed soldiers and a total of twenty two Irish people but these were only a part of the scene. The payments to soldiers cease after 1656 and do not appear again until 1660 but in the meantime there are a great number of payments to seaman and sailors. One in 1657 '...lost his Shipp and Goods...' and received 8d from the parish. The lack of payments to soldiers may reflect a certain disenchantment with the army during this period; although an Elizabethan statute had ensured the 'necessary relief of soldiers and sailors' by churchwardens in the parishes throughout the country.[47] A few years later, in 1661, there occurs a payment for the largest single item, 16s for 'drawing the Kyngs Armes'. This presumably relates to the creation of the first standing army under Charles II.

In 1653 payments were made to 'two poore women whose husbands were taken by the turke...', similarly in 1658 payments were made to three women. In between a poor man that '...came out of Turkey' received assistance. Similar troubles with the 'Turks' are recorded at Winchester.[48] Stories concerning difficulties with foreigners seemed to evoke sympathy, for two seaman 'taken by the Ostenders' received 3d in 1658 whilst a poor man robbed by the Spaniards a year earlier received the same amount. In 1654 and 1660 there are several mentions of payments to people merely described as 'Travellers'. It is possible that these were amongst the earliest of the Gypsies to frequent the parish.

Payments made to those who suffered a loss by fire were not uncommon, though in one entry of 1653 double sympathy is evident in that a payment was made to '8 cripples [who had] loss by fire' though they only received 6d. The ever present risk of fire, in an era where timber framed, thatched cottages was the norm, is clear from these and many similar entries. The problems of natural disaster had evoked the sympathy of Parliament, for the churchwardens were required to assist those who suffered loss through fire or misfortune at sea.[49]

Fig 34 **Honey-suckle Cottage Tearooms after a disastrous fire on 18th March 1999 serves as a reminder of the dangers inherent in thatched and timber buildings**

A note written in the account book the following year explains clearly the position of the churchwardens and the collective attitude of the parish:-

> ...whereas the sayd Churchwardens [Andrew Nash and Phillip Ansell] have been lumbered in a sute of Law about Robert Lambe and were overthrown therein they having been elected by the Parishoners I think in equity and good consciencs they ought to be protected and kept harme-lesse by them...

There is evidence in the succeeding year that the wardens did recoup some, at least, of their money.

Consecutive entries for 1654 are tantalising:-

> It[em] for a warrant for Robert Hobbs 0[s] 6[d]
> It[em] for a warrant to stop the execution 1[s] 0[d]

The two items may not be linked. No further information about the warrant for Robert Hobbs has been found. Whatever the issue Hobbs (or his namesake) did not seem to be endeared with or loved by his neighbours. In 1673 he was presented for the erection of a cottage before an inquisition into wastes and spoils of the Forest. Four years later at a similar inquiry, assisted by his sister, Edith Osmand, he got his own back by indicting a dozen or so of their neighbours with various Forest misdemeanours as described earlier.[50]

The later warrant could well relate to a murder case that came before the Western Circuit Assizes at Winchester that year. Judith Blake and Anne Piball of Bartley were accused by Thomas Bowman, John Crowcher, and Thomas Heathcock, all of Bartley, of killing the former's husband.[51] The result is unknown except to say that ten years later an Ann Pyball is living at Bartley three properties away from 'Blaks Cottages'.[52] One of the three accusers, Crowcher, actually lived at London Minstead. When he died in 1661 he was financially ruined: the person to whom he owed most money was one 'Widow Pyball of Ealing'.[53]

Phillip Ansell the Churchwarden of 1653 was required to fetch a warrant and later claimed expenses in '...goeing after John Bidlecombe...'. Biddlecombe, a former member of the vestry committee, disappeared from the scene and is not recorded further in the parish.

The following item from 1655 is typical of a large number of entries, though showing more detail than most.

> It[em] to poore people t[ha]t came for a collection as it was consented unto by officers and neighbours of the parish 2s 2d

A brief, which was an authorized collection for charitable purposes, papal in origin but following the reformation designated 'Royal', is rarely mentioned in Minstead. The two earliest recorded are payments of one shilling in 1660 and of one shilling and sixpence to 'lodging of men that had a breaffe...' the following year. The second entry indicates the nature of the system. It was the practice to read out the details of the brief during the service and at the end the clerk would take the collection by the church door. Funds raised in this manner were then passed onto the travelling collector.[54] This equivalent to the more recent 'Sunday television appeal' was abolished in 1828 after much concern about misuse in the previous century.

Many of the wills, particularly those of the first half of the 17th century showed concern for the poor of the village, money often being bequeathed for their benefit. The number leaving money in this way drops as the century proceeds, perhaps because of the perception that the poor will now be looked after by the parish. On occasion it would seem that animate objects were left for the benefit of the parish. In 1641 and 1650 Christopher Stride paid 4s to the churchwardens for the use of a cow, three others were looked after by Robert Over, Robert Soffe and John Croucher in 1652.

Bell ringing as a cause of celebration is a frequent cost to the parish not only for assistance to the ringers who were encouraged with ale but also for the repairs that often seemed to follow. Impartiality was clearly the keynote to survival in difficult times as two entries show. In 1660 the parish was still celebrating the discovery of the gunpowder plot, three shillings was paid to the ringers, whose good work no doubt caused the next entry: one shilling and eight pence to Drew Penton for mending the bells. The following year the same pattern is followed with three shillings and sixpence to the ringers and a requirement for two new bell ropes. The difference is that on the second occasion the celebration was the anniversary of Charles II's coronation.

Entries in 1657 and 1658 relate to recusants, Richard Compton had taken the oath of abjuration in 1657 but wasn't the only Catholic associated with the parish. Six others, all from Canterton, were presented at Quarter Sessions that year for being 'popishly affected'.[55] In the Compton census of 1676 nine people were listed as papists and eight as nonconformists.[56]

The church tower required attention in 1641 and again in 1656. In the later year quite substantial repairs were made to the timber work; this is the predecessor to the present tower. In the former year work was also needed on 'nayles and other iron worke about the Bells...' this may be fitting of the bell marked IH (John Higden) cast in 1638.[57]

The porch to the church was added in 1683 and bears the letters REWSCW; unfortunately the churchwardens accounts are not extant for that year so the names of the church wardens cannot be given with any certainty. However

Richard Ecton and William Stride are two likely candidates with William Soffe and William Seward as other possibilities.

A reference to an almshouse built by Sir Henry Compton at some time before 1635 in the East Bailiwick could relate to his property held at Exbury or Lepe though the Bailiwick does stretch north west as far as Ashurst.[58] Establishing an almshouse was not at all an uncommon practice in the century preceding the Civil War.[59] Although Minstead is not within that bailiwick it is possible that those in need were able to obtain relief there. Compton had great experience of such places for he was assistant warden at Sackville College in East Grinstead in 1628 and continued his work there until 1642 by which time he had troubles of his own.[60]

CHURCH MAINTENANCE

Repairs to the church roof, although often of little more than parochial interest, do in fact reveal a great deal about the local economy. The accounts show what materials were used, where they came from, who carried them and the costs involved. Details of procedures to obtain timber from the Forest are recorded along with the costs of setting up rails around the churchyard.

Repairs to the church windows are mentioned half a dozen times though the process used is only shown once. In 1653 an amount of three shillings and four pence is costed against glazing the windows, the next item, of a shilling, is for a fire for the same purpose. The bells needed frequent attention, often in conjunction with the tower. A bell wheel fitted in 1641, may have required removal of part of the framework of the tower to fit it. The work that year cost twenty one shillings and two pence (though part of the document is missing) which included ten shillings for the bell wheel. Fifteen years later the sum of thirty four shillings and two pence was spent on work within the church; of this five shillings and six pence went on glazing the windows, the remainder on repairing the tower and bells. A local man, Thomas Godden, carried out much of the work on the tower and was paid five shillings for his services.

Repairs to the roof in 1646 show that it was already tiled then. Further fairly major repairs were made in 1658, mostly to the roof. Masons from Romsey were employed at a cost of nineteen shillings and two pence, five hundred tiles were bought for seven shillings and six pence and, curiously just two ridging tiles for eight pence. The tiles were bought along with lime from Redlynch,

Clement Morris fetching them. Sand was procured by another local man, John Croucher. (Perhaps this was the origin of 'Crouchers hole' in Castle Malwood Walk mentioned in the inquiry of 1677?)[61] There being no reliable message service the Churchwarden (either William Burgis or Robert Soffe) had to make journeys to Romsey to enlist the masons and to Redlynch to order materials not available locally. Laths and nails used in the work were probably made nearby, over twelve hundred of the latter were used, which would have kept the blacksmith busy for quite a spell.

Five years later a further three pounds eight shillings and sixpence was spent on church repairs. Again much of this seems to have been on roof repairs, with a sheet of lead being purchased together with three hundred laths. Other timber (a ton and a half) and over a hundred boards imply quite substantial work. A small number of bricks were also bought, these were collected by William Burgess along with the lime. The lime came from Toothill as did 4,000 nails on this occasion. A variety of nail sizes were used costing anything from just under a penny a hundred to one shilling a hundred. Two quarters of lime was costed at eight shillings with its carriage adding another four shillings.

1649 saw major expenditure on railings around the church yard. The whole process is explained in some detail from the churchwardens visit to the magistrate, Mr Hildesley, to obtain the timber from the Forest through to a note of who dug the holes for the post (Simon Hussey). Exactly what authority Hildesley had in the Forest is not known, he was a local landowner from Hinton, a supporter of Parliament who became Sheriff of the county in 1657. He is noted as holding 'diverse records concerning the forest' in 1670 and appears as a commissioner of an inquiry into the wastes and spoils of the New Forest in 1673.[62] When permission had been obtained Edward Wright felled the timber, 'Goodman' (either Thomas or Richard) Godwine was responsible for 'squareinge and breakinge' it and Phillip Ansell carried it to the churchyard. Once there a saw pit was dug in which Richard Godden and his assistant had the unenviable task of producing five hundred rails and posts, a job which took them the best part of a week. At least the village pub was close by to slake their thirst.

CHURCH POSSESSIONS

When the churchwardens completed their term of office they had to note the amounts either owing or being paid to their successors. Francis House and John Seward in 1649 also listed the church goods when they handed over to Thomas

Brown and Michael Archer. These included a chalice with a cover, a flaggon, a pulpit cushion and cloth, a Bible, a chest and a carpet for the table.

A note of the glebe lands belonging to the parsonage was made in 1663. There were four acres together with a dwelling house, barn, outhouses and 'backside'.[63]

THE TRUSTY SERVANT

Although little direct reference to the village pub is made in the 17th century records, it is clearly extant by implication and confirmed by a 19th century document. A tenant of the manor, John Caull, is required to attend to a ditch at the '...end of Long close by innbridge...'[64] Similarly an adjacent field was held by Call's neighbour, John Purckis, in 1652.[65] A dwelling called interchangeably Innbridge or Dunbridge occurs in the rates list from the 1690's, then in the occupation of the Purkiss family. The present Dunbridge Cottage occupies this site opposite *The Trusty Servant* and close to the stream course. A schedule of properties changing hands in 1837 includes:

> ...A public house called the Trusty Servant situate at Minsteed in the County of Southampton held by lease dated the tenth of December One Thousand six hundred and two for the residue of a term of One thousand years at the yearly rent of a pepper corn in the occupation of [gap left].[66]

ROADS

The basic pattern of roads and tracks to and through Minstead in the 17th century is shown on the map. Much, of course, must be speculative based upon fragments found in the records. The odd present day survival of names helps the process. 'Pylmore gate' at the west side of the manor is one of three gate names mentioned in 1565. Another, 'Rode gate', also in Fritham Bailiwick, is mentioned immediately after Acres Down and before Pilmore Gate. Red Open Ford (GR SU278095) fits well with this description and is shown on the first edition OS 6" map of 1870. The entries, though not in strict geographical order, are grouped indicating their rough position. 'Purkesgate' is shown to be close to Hazel Hill in the North Bailiwick.[67] The hill is north east of Minstead Lodge so the gate could refer to either the approach to the manor near Perry's Farm or Football Green. The latter seems more likely, for a property at the western end of Football Green, as it narrows, belonged to Aaron Purkess in 1787.[68] 'Foales Gate' or Foolsgate on the O.S. 1st edition but now Foldsgate (GR SU295093)

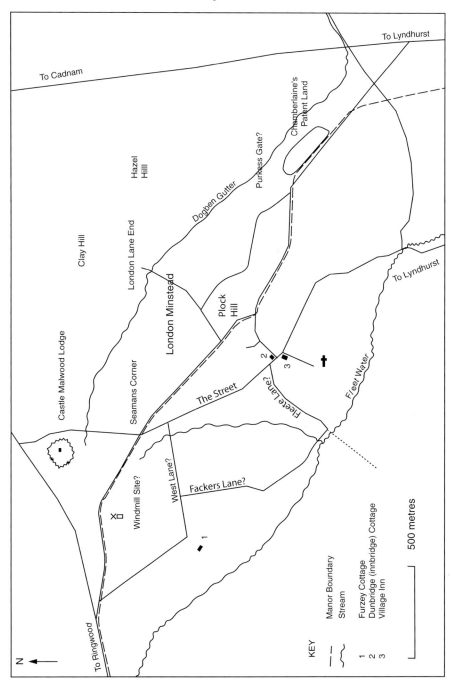

Fig 35 Composite map of Minstead in the 17th century, see text for details

appears in a forest document of 1615.[69] Some names have changed with time; the road from *The Trusty Servant* along the southern edge of Cauldrons and up the hill, now Bull Lane, was once called Plockhill. Known as 'plucley lane' in 1609 it provided a winding link between Minstead and the properties which formerly stood close to the present Minstead Lodge site at London Minstead.[70] The unmade road which now leads to a footpath on the western side of Cauldrons was Hobbs Lane so named because it led to a property owned by Robert Hobbs.[71] A property still stood on that site in the 19th century. The footpath was termed the 'Church path' in 1735 providing a shorter (and perhaps less muddy) route from London Minstead than the road.

At the north of the village, running through Malwood is the old road from Romsey to Ringwood. The section passing through Minstead appears to have changed little since Roman times, part of the boundary of the Manor is aligned along its southern edge and would have greatly assisted communications between Minstead and Bisterne. The two Manors had been linked in ownership since at least the time of Edward the Confessor. That road ran past the iron age earthwork, Castle Malwood, which in turn appears to have had a road linking it directly to Lyndhurst. Travelling south east it followed the existing road past the village green as far as what is now Park Farm and continued, slightly east of south, over the stream. From there it carried on past the western edge of Harcourt Wood and up Burnt Hill to join the road between Emery Down and the Kennels (Mill Lane) close by the stream. It then followed the footpath over the stream through a field to the open forest where is can be clearly seen, deep cut, running uphill to emerge between Bunkers Hill and the allotments. The existing road to Pikes Hill and on to Lyndhurst is the obvious continuation. This route, possibly in existence for two thousand years, was stopped up at the request of Henry Combe Compton, Lord of the Manor in 1814. The present indirect route leading out to the Cadnam - Lyndhurst road was substituted.[72]

Boundary stones of both the manor and the parish help to provide clues to positions of old roads. Whilst the stones prime purpose is to denote the boundary they do not occur at regular intervals. Their placing is usually made for one of two reasons, either to mark a change in alignment or to show that a boundary is being crossed to a user of a road or track.

A further lane, no longer in use, is indicated on the tithe map of 1842. Starting from where the previously mentioned road crossed the Fleet water in Manor Park (GR SU286104) this ran in a north easterly direction. A short section of it may still be seen past the recently renovated Mill Lane cottage situated between Williams Hill and Mill Farm (GR SU291103). After following a field hedge it emerged from the Manor onto the Forest at a point still marked by a boundary stone (GR SU294105). It can be traced on the ground for a few hundred metres, eventually crossing the modern Cadnam to Lyndhurst road. Where it leaves the parish there is a stone dated 1822 with MP on one side and EP for Eling parish on the other (GR SU297107). The northern bank of Furzey Lawn Inclosure (made around 1775) follows its line alongside Dogben Gutter and would then presumably have continued onto Woodlands or Bartley. Parts of it are still clearly shown on the 1st edition 6" to one mile Ordnance Survey map surveyed around 1870.

Other alterations to roads include the route from Castle Malwood to Football Green; it originally ran through the grounds of Minstead Lodge to the south of the present building emerging onto the green close to the cricket pavilion. School Lane was obviously only so named in the 19th century when the School was built but could be the West Lane referred to in the 1690's. It seems more likely that it was 'Fackers Lane' mentioned on a number of occasions in the court records.[73] Another possibility for West Lane is the one from Minstead Hut to Furzey Cottage, the high banks as it mounts the hill indicates it is of some age, it has had at least two old cottages alongside it in the past (GR SU275115).[74] Fleet Lane mentioned in 1653 seems to run from the present Wisteria Cottage over the ford to Newtown.[75] Seamans Lane is the natural boundary between the crown lands of Lyndhurst Manor and those of the Compton's Minstead Manor. Its present line is not quite as it was even two centuries ago, part of the property occupied by Wembdon Cottage appears to have encroached into the lane. At the junction by Bull Lane, Yew Tree Cottage also looks to be built into the road of the time but would have been constructed before the Minstead Lodge diversion. At the other end, Seamans Corner was used as a meeting place for beating the bounds at Whitsun, 1653. Robert Over junior held Seaman's at London Minstead in 1666 so the name has been in use long before either *The New Inn* (Eugenie Cottage) or *The Royal Oak* (Hungerford Cottage) were established in the 18th and 19th centuries respectively. The name may originate with J Seman, a Forest Officer in the reign of Henry VI.[76] Whilst this could be thought to dispel the old story of the lane being used by the press gang, an item in the churchwardens accounts of 1666 for two shillings paid to '...8 sholgers in the conveing of prest men two Portmuth' leaves room for thought as to how such tales start.

The road out of Manor Park past North Lodge heading to French's Bushes is likely to be of 19th century date linked to the expansion of the Manor House and grounds after the Comptons settled in the village having sold Bisterne in 1792. Close to its junction with the lane that joins it, heading towards Bartley from London Minstead, is a parish boundary stone dated 1750 (GR SU294121). 'Lane end next my house' is indicated in a will of 1584 for a property that stood on land opposite Perrys Farm and at least implies the beginnings of a way across the forest past this stone to Bartley.[77] This may be close to the 'Newlands End' which was one side of fifteen acres of oak mentioned in 1565, it was bounded by 'Dagbournes' [Dogben gutter] at the other end. 'Newlands End' whilst not being conclusive at least indicates the latest date at which some of the lands at London Minstead were enclosed.[78]

Notes

1 HRO 1599A21A/1-2 Joan Currington
2 D Vick, *West Hants Lay Subsidy Assessments 1558-1603*, pp. 71-2
3 HRO 1627AD37/1-2 John King
4 HRO 1639A138/1-2 John King
5 HRO 1641A110/1-2 John Stride
6 HRO 90M71/PW1, Minstead Churchwardens Accounts
7 HRO Q4/1 Indictment Book 1646-1660
8 CB Oct 1653
9 HRO 1639A138/2 John Kinge
10 HRO 1670AD028 Robert Burgess
11 PRO E 178/6453, Inquiry, 1677
12 *CSP Dom.* 1670 p. 97
13 HRO 13M64/35
14 See Appendix 3
15 HRO 1697A33/1 Ruth Cull
16 HRO 1667AO23/2 John Chater
17 HRO 1616B85/1-2 Thomas Malie
18 HRO 1623A56/1-4 Edward Moulton
19 HRO 1627AD37/2 John Kinge
20 HRO 1641A110/1-2 John Stride
21 HRO 1679A139/1-2 William Stride
22 HRO 1629A15/1 Gilbert Canon; HRO 1634B22/1-2 Richard Hobbs
23 HRO 1639A138 John Kinge; HRO 1638AD086 James Goldfinch
24 HRO 1641A110/1-2 John Stride
25 HRO 1636A34 Robert Henvest; HRO 1653AD11/2 Thomas Friend
26 PRO E 179/247/30

27 Hughes and White, 1991, op. cit., p. vii
28 Hughes and White, 1991, op. cit., pp. vii-viii
29 HRO 5M53/739
30 PRO LRRO 5/39 Taverner's Survey
31 HRO 1584A34/1-2 William Hobbes; C R Davey, *The Hampshire Lay Subsidy Rolls, 1586*, Hampshire Record Series, Winchester, 1981, 303
32 Stagg, 1983, op. cit., pp. x-xi, 1577; See J Thirsk, The Crown as projector... pp. 320-6 in R W Hoyle *The Estates of the English Crown 1558-1640*, Cambridge, 1992, for interpretation.
33 Stagg, 1983, op. cit., 626-7, 630
34 HRO 5M53/739 Court Rolls of Wriothesley Manors 1626-31 - Lindhurst pp. 41a - 43b
35 HRO 1661A27/1-3 John Croucher
36 *Claims, 1670*, op. cit., 155, 266
37 HRO 1618B34 Christpian Kember
38 Statute 43 Eliz. I c 2
39 Statute 14 Car. II c 12
40 HRO 90M71/PW1, Minstead Churchwardens Accounts
41 J B Black, *The Reign of Elizabeth 1558-1603*, Oxford, 2nd edition 1959, p. 409; G. Davies, *The Early Stuarts*, Oxford, 1937, pp. 61, 231-2
42 HRO 24M82/PO16/42
43 HRO 24M82/PO33/2
44 J Richardson, *The Local Historian's Encyclopedia*, 1974, 1986 edition, D47
45 Ordinance, 24 Aug 1653
46 Statute 26 Hen. VIII, c 3
47 Statute 43 Eliz. I c 3
48 W A Fearon and J F Williams, *The Parish Registers and Parochial Documents in the Archdeaconry of Winchester*, Winchester, 1909, pp. 58-9
49 Statute 43 Eliz. I c 2, s 15
50 PRO E 178/6453, Inquiry, 1677
51 PRO ASSI 24/1, Bail book of Western Circuit Assizes 1653-1677
52 Hughes and White, 1991, op. cit., p. 57
53 HRO 1661A27/1-3 John Croucher
54 W E Tate, *The Parish Chest*, 1946, 3rd ed 1969, p. 120
55 HRO QX1/10 Quarter Session Indictments and presentments 1646-1660, p. 74
56 Whitehead, 1986, op. cit. p. 90
57 *Church guide*, nd
58 Stagg, 1983, op. cit., 648
59 E M Leonard, *The Early History of English Poor Relief*, Cambridge, 1900, p. 210
60 WSRO Add. Ms. 17,842; Eric C Byford, *Aspects of the History of Brambletye, Forest Row*, Vol 4 Pt 3 p. 23, the College was more like an almshouse, rather than a college as would be described today.
61 PRO E 178/6453, Inquiry, 1677

62 King, 1879, p. 242; Henning, 1983, op. cit., Vol 2 pp. 548-9; Stagg, 1983, op. cit., 1471; PRO E 178/6453
63 HRO 35M48 16/275 Glebe Terrier of Minstead
64 CFP Apr 1652
65 CFP Oct 1652
66 HRO 11M59/E2/286240
67 PRO LRRO 5/39, Taverner's Survey
68 PRO F 17/250; F 20/48
69 PRO E 178/3097 m.32
70 PRO E/147/6/11
71 HRO 70M87/8 Indenture between William Olding and John Kent
72 HRO Q1/30 88, Quarter Session Book
73 CB Oct 1653, Mar 1654, Oct 1654
74 PRO IR 30/31/177 Minstead Tithe map, 1842
75 CB April 1653
76 PRO E 101/142/9
77 HRO 1584A34 William Hobbs
78 PRO LRRO 5/39 Taverner's Survey

Postscript

Much that has been brought out by this survey of a 17th century Forest village was self evident: a pastoral village rather than an arable one because of limited productive land and therefore little need to regulate agriculture. Although the Manorial services had all but gone, the traditions of working together, that the courts still provided, maintained a form of cohesion for the community. Commoning was not a full time way of life, I doubt that it ever was. There were a few larger farms but many people relied on two occupations - one of them commoning. There was little paid work in the village for there was only a small amount of the manorial lords land to tend. The use of wood based industries alongside forest commoning allowed many a form of independence on a scale perhaps unknown in many southern counties. With the enclosure and sale of almost all the other Royal Forests the New Forest provides an opportunity for studying a system which survived virtually unimpaired until the early part of the twentieth century. Commoning still survives, albeit wilfully, to provide the link between families and generations that has been lost in most parts of the country.

For the researcher there has been a number of finds, some of which have been of importance to understanding the working of the community. The existence of a windmill built in the middle of the century was unknown at the outset. Research elsewhere in the county suggests that these were far more widely used than was thought even twenty five years ago. Important, in terms of Forest research but not perhaps parish, was the discovery of the site of a 14th century king's hunting lodge, Harborough, at Bolderwood. Similarly the discovery that the so called Regarders Returns, a widely used source of information on the Elizabethan Forest in fact denoted the records of a previously unknown (in the New Forest) exchequer officer called a Preservator proved interesting. More than anything though was the gradual, if only partial, understanding of what was important in the lives of villagers through reading their wills and inventories.

The social links reflected in the wills and the court rolls show a community, on the whole, working together with similar concerns and regard of property that was vital to all. The way that the villagers and the forest officers rubbed along together suggests, for the most part, a mutual respect. Anyone who has worked on a farm or attended a drift understands the need for neighbours to work together. An independently minded community that understood mutuality - is this an anomaly or has it been a recipe for survival?

Appendix I
Inventories and wills used

Hampshire Record Office reference number and name:-

1578A50/2	John Pinhorne
1584A34/1-2	William Hobbes
1591B19/1-2	Nicholas Donington
1592B57/1-2	Stephen Trussler
1595AD45	Robert Purques
1597AD51	John Hobbs
1599A21A/1-2	Jone Curringtone
1599A48/1-2	Richard Lovill
1601A7/1-2	Rychard Barton
1603A45/1-2	William Purkes
1612B52/1-2	John Kippin
1616B85/1-2	Thomas Malie [Macie?]
1617AD8	Rychard Baerline
1620A68/1-2	Clement Peirce
1623A56/1-4	Edward Moulton
1623AD96	Edward Willoughby
1625A87/1-2	John Moresh
1627AD37/1-2	John Kinge
1627AD60	Edward Ranger
1629A15/1-2	Gilbert Canon
1631AD94	Phillip Stride
1632A9/1	George Barton
1634B22/1-2	Richard Hobbs
1634AD07/1	George Bright
1636A34/1-2	Robert Henvest
1638AD086	James Goldfinch
1639A138/1-2	John Kinge
1641A54/1-2	John Hobbs
1641A110/1-2	John Stride
1650AD32	Simon Hussey
1653AD11/1-2	Thomas Friend
1653A7/1-2	Alice Friend
1661A27/1-3	John Croucher
1662AD45	Jacob Hayes
1665A94/1-2	Dorothy Rice
1665AD99	Philip Stride
1666A68/1-2	James Phillips
1667A23/1-2	John Chater

1668A72/1-2	Ann Purcas
1668B32	Francis Howse
1671AD55	William Gaine
1676AD74	John Lewyn
1677AD89	Drew Penton
1679A139/1-2	William Stride
1679A156	William Whitcher
1681A131	John Purkis
1682AD50	Joan King
1683AD80	John Purcas
1687B16/1-3	Clement Mores
1695AD79/1-2	Crisan Whicher
1697A33/1-2	Ruth Cull

The list includes Thomas and Alice Friend who died within days of each other. As these were virtually identical only one inventory was used.

Appendix II
Sample Inventories

It is impossible to select 'typical' inventories covering a period of over a century; these
have been selected to link with the cattle ownership figures in chapter 4.
1-5 cattle Edward Moulton 1623
6-10 cattle Joan Currington 1599
11-15 cattle John Chater 1665
16 plus cattle William Hobbs, 1584

Comprehension is sometimes helped by reading aloud in the local accent.

Two versions of Edward Moulton's inventory exist, the earlier is listed first.

HRO 1623A56/3

A enmetore tacken of the tru and last [will] of edward moulton
his weareng parell six shelenges 8d
too keene forty shelenges and ten gratas
too steeres boollokes at tharti shelenges
won hefear bolock fife sheleng
won mare ayghtane shelenges
won acre of heay four nobueles
won kobord tan grates
wodun housheulstuf ten shelenges
pautur and brass sex tene shelages
the beden at fife she lenges
the iaron stuf twelfe peanes

the sum of thes en metore [inventory] es 8l 8s
Christopher Stride [signed and writer]
humfare wasse hes marck
John pearces hes marcke

HRO 1623A56/4

A trew inventorie of all the goods of Edward Moulton late of the parish of Minsteed
in the county of South[ampton] colier deceased, as they were praysed by Christopher
Stride Humphry Wisse and Jhon Peirse

Imprimis his waring apparell		6s	8d
Twoe kine	£2	3s	4d
Twoe steer bullocks	£1	10s	

One Haekfer bullocke		5s	
One Mare		18s	
One reake of Hey	£1	6s	8d
One Cubbord		3s	4d
Wooden houshold stufe		10s	
Pewter and brasse		16s	
Bedinge		5s	
Iron stuffe			12d

Summa totalis is £8   8s

Debts that were owinge unto the sayd Edward Moulton deceased are these

Henry Mereman the elder	40s	
Richard Zeager	5s	
Nicolas Cob	7s	6d

Notes

The total should be £8 5s; the 3s subtotal from the pence column appears to have been added twice.

There are two versions of both Moulton's will and inventory. The later versions of each are in the same hand and have added to them in a second (contemporary) hand a note stating that it is but a copy of the original.

HRO 1599A21A/2 Jone Curringtone

[In margin] Mynsteed
[In margin] Anno 1599
The trew Inventorie of all the goodes and Cattall [of all the goodes and C crossed out] of Jone Curringtone widowe deceassed the iiijth of Novembe praysed the vth of [Decemb crossed out] Novembe by Thomas burgis, Richard Spenser and Rychard Emerie

Apparrell

Imp[rim]is her Apparrell and clothes   xxs

Chamber

Item one Beedsteed, one feather beed and ij Coverlettes, iij^{re} blankettes ij payer of sheetes   xxvjs viijd

Item iiij^{or} coffers   viijs

The hale

Item xij peaces of pewter	viijs
Item v Candelstickes	ijs viijd
Item one brasse panne v kettelles ij skillettes one pott	xxxs
Item one Table bord ij stoles one forme	
one stayned clothe and Benches	vjs viijd
Item one broche ij wedges one pothengers	
one Andirone and other smale Iron thinges	iijs iiijd
Item the Trine vessell and shelffes	xs

['Item' crossed out]

Cattall

Item nine kine	xili	
Item iij hogges		xxvis viijd
Item thirtie fower Beestales	vijli	vs
Item one gold ringe		xxs
Item monnie	iiijli	

| S[u]mma Totalis | xxxli | xjs |

Notes

The total should be £30 7s 0d

HRO 1667A23/2 John Chater

A trew and p[er]fect Inventory of all and singuler the goodes and chattles late of John Chater of London Minstead in the County of Sout[hamp]t[on] Carpent[er] deceased taken the Tenth day of Aprill Anno D[o]m[ini] 1667 by those whose names are under written as followeth

Imprimis his wareing apparell all given to John Chater and Thomas Symonds by will
£2 0s 0d
Item his workeing Tooles all given to William Chater   £0 5s 0d
Item Twelve kine and heifers and one weaneling calfe all given to Charity his wif att
£16 05s 0d
Item one Nagge given alsoe to the s[ai]d Charity   £1 00s 0d

Item Five Piggs given alsoe to her   £1 0s 0d
Item Twoe sheepe given alsoe to her   £0 5s 0d
Item Twoe stocks of bees given her   £0 10s 0d
Item the Household stuff all given to the s[ai]d Charity his relict as followeth Twoe beds
and all that belongs to them £4 all the Pewter and Brass xxviiis all the Linnen vs all the
woodden vessells xs one cubbord and one Borde vs chairs shelvs and forms vs Books
3s 4d chests and Cofers and other Lumber xvs   £7 11s 4d
Item a Lease of a smale Cottage in Fordingbridg   £2 0s 0d
Item the Lease of the Mills att North Ashly given to William Chater his sonne
                                                                      £60 0s 0d
Total sume is   £90 16s 4d

the m[ar]ke of Edward Knowles   }
                                } Apprezos
the m[ar]ke of Wm Stride   }

HRO 1584A34/1-2 William Hobbs

A trewe Inventorie of all the goodes and cattaill of william hobbes of the paryshe of
minsteed disceased the xvith daye of September praised by John [hobbes crossed out]
henvest, Richard truslor and stephen truslor the xxviiith of Septemb[e]r

The hale

Imp[rim]us all suche stuffe and Implemetes as arre in the hale moveable
                                                        xxvjs   viijd

The chamber

Item his wearinge Apparrell   xxs
Item all suche stuffe and Implemetes as arre in the Chamber moveable
                                                        xls

Kychine

Item all suche Implemetes as arre in the Kychine   vjs   viijd

his good without the dore

Ite[m] his hey   iijli   vjs   viijs
Ite[m] his ColeFier wood   xvjs

his Cattaile

Item xij kine	xijli		
Ite[m] two steres		xls	
Item xi bullockes of three yeares of age	vjli	vjs	viijd
Ite[m] vij bullockes of ayeare old and moore	iijli	xs	
Ite[m] v wenelinge calves		xxvs	

his horse beastes

Ite[m] one old nagge and iiii coltes	iijli	vjs	viijd
Ite[m] two old mares		xls	
Ite[m] iij^re tegg coltes and one old mare		xxxs	

his hogges

Ite[m] vii old hogges of the age of ayeare and one quarter		xxviijs	
Ite[m] xvij yonger hogges of one yeare old		liijs	viijd
Ite[m] v yonger of the age of halffe ayeare		xs	
Ite[m] xj wenelinge pigges		xiiijs	viijd
Ite[m] iiij yonge^r pigges		iiijs	
sums	xlvjli	iiijs	viijd

Appendix III
Occupations and descriptions noted in Minstead

Blacksmith
James Goldfinch, 1638

Browser
____ Gregory browser to Gauntlet of Castle Malwood Walk, 1677 Inquiry

Carpenter
John Hobbs, 1597
Richard Lovell of Dowlehayes house carpenter, 1599
Richard Barton carpenter, 1601
John Chater Carpenter, 1667

Charcoal Burner
John Pinhorne collier, 1578
Henry Cobb collyer of M, aged 25, 1615 Depositions
James Cobb of M, 1615 Depositions
Nicholas Cobbe of Mynsteed, Collyer, aged 30, 1615 Depositions
Phillip Stride, aged 55, 1615 Depositions
Edward Moulton collier, 1623
Richard Hobbs, 1634
Christopher Stride charcoal burner of M, DJS 1634 411
William Cobb charcoal burner of M, DJS 1635 621
Edward Hobbs charcoal burner of M, DJS 1635 616
John Hobbs charcoal burner of M, DJS 1635 729
John Purcas charcoal burner of LM and M, DJS 1635 504, 770
John Eldridge Collier, 1677 Inquiry
George Howse collier, 1677 Inquiry
William Purcas of Minsteed collier, 1677 Inquiry
Thomas Soffe collier, 1677 Inquiry
William Stride of London Minsteed collier, 1677 Inquiry
Richard Symonds collier, 1677 Inquiry
John Pukas collier, 1681
John Purkiss Collier, 1683

Cooper
Gersian? Gird of M aged 30, 1615 Depositions

Fusterer
John Robbynes of Mynsteed, Foysterer, aged 35, 1615 Depositions
John Wright fusterer of M, DJS 1635 624

Edward Wright fusterer of M, DJS 1636 410
William Wright of M a sadletree maker, 1677 Inquiry

Gentleman
John Roberts gentleman, DJS 1634 300
Thomas Browne gentleman of LM tenant of Lyndhurst Manor, DJS 1635 492
Morgan Haynes gentleman of London Minstead, DJS 1635 456

Husbandman
Nicholas Donnington husbandman, 1591
John Kinge husbandman of M aged 36, 1602 PRO E 101/2047 ms.16
Richard piers husbandman of M aged 50, 1602 PRO E 101/2047 ms.16
Richard Baerline husbandman, 1617
Clement Peirce husbandman, 1620
Thomas Woolfe Husbandman of M, DJS 1634 340
Richard Corbin husbandman of M, DJS 1635 609
Thomas Hobbs husbandman of LM, DJS 1635 608
Thomas Marshman husbandman of M, DJS 1635 625
Madelin Michell husbandman of M, DJS 1635 622
Richard Osman husbandman of M, DJS 1635 729
William Osman husbandman deceased Canterton, DJS 1635 623
John Paynter husbandman of M, DJS 1635 630
John Peirce son of Richard Peirce husbandman of M, DJS 1635 729
Robert Whitehorne husbandman of M, DJS 1635 613
James Goldfinch husbandman/blacksmith, 1638
John Hobbs husbandman, 1641
Thomas Freind Husbandman, 1653

Keeper
Michaell Cawle of Harberough Lodge, aged 50, 1615 Depositions
Edward Ranger keeper, 1627
George Bright yeoman/underforester, 1634
John Lewyn Keeper/Gent, 1676
___ Gauntlet keeper of Castle Malwood Walk, 1677 Inquiry

Labourer
Edward Booth of M aged 32, 1615 Depositions
Thomas Johnson deceased of M, 1615 Depositions
Simon Hussey labourer of M, DJS 1633 336
Thomas Woolfe labourer of M, DJS 1634 410
Richard Osman labourer of M, DJS 1635 629
John Paynter labourer of M, DJS 1635 626
John Pearce jun son of Richard Pearce labourer of M, DJS 1635 620

Miller
Drew Penton Miller, 1677 Inquiry

Property Developer
William Olding, 1677 Inquiry

Ranger
Edward Willoughby ranger, 1609 Salisbury (Cecil) Mss 132 126, DJS 1622 App B
Thomas Browne gentleman, DJS 1635 262

Sawyer
Thomas Buckle employed by Wm Olding, 1677 Inquiry
John Henvest employed by Wm Olding, 1677 Inquiry

Servant
John Horne the elder, 1599A21A/1 Jone Currington
Richard Osmond Emanuell Osmond [gap] Somers amd Michaell Whithorn servants
(labourers) of Eldrige, 1677 Inquiry

Shoemaker
John Millis shoemaker of M, DJS 1635 618
John Kinge, 1639

Tailor
Richard Hayes tailor of M, DJS 1635 611
Thomas Rogers, DJS 1635 770
John Stride, HRO 24M82/PO16/42, 1671

Timber Carrier
William Olding, 1677 Inquiry

Timber Dealer
Robert Cull, 1677 Inquiry
John Martin of LM, 1677 Inquiry
Robert Over of LM, 1677 Inquiry

Upholtsterer
Richard Cull, in 1627AD37/1-2 (John Kinge)

Weaver
Robert Henvest weaver, 1636

Woodward of Minstead
Michael Call senior, DJS 1635 276, 1622 App B
Robert Soff, DJS 1660-8 App B
Ellis Weekes, DJS 1669 App B

Yeoman
John Kippin yeoman, 1612
John Kinge yeoman, 1627
Christopher Stride yeoman of M, DJS 1633 334
George Bright yeoman underforester of Malwood Lodge, DJS 1634 327
Thomas Frinde of M yeoman, DJS 1634 303
John Burden yeoman of M, DJS 1635 615
John Chater yeoman of M, DJS 1635 456
John Crowcher yeoman of LM, DJS 1635 770
John Pearce yeoman deceased of M, DJS 1635 610
John Ventam yeoman of M, DJS 1635 766
John Stride yeoman, 1641

Sources

A date on its own after a name refers to the named persons will or inventory, see appendix I for details.
DJS (year) followed by numbers refers to D J Stagg, *A Calendar of New Forest Documents 15th to 17th centuries*, Hampshire Record Series Vol V, 1983, Winchester.
1615 Depositions PRO E178/3097 m.32&33 Depositions taken concerning John Norden's sale of trees in the New Forest, dated 11 & 21 April (13 Jas.I).
1677 Inquiry PRO E 178 6453 Commission of Inquiry.
M is Minstead; LM is London Minstead.

Notes

A browser would have been employed in providing appropriate greenery from the forest for feeding the deer.
A fusterer was a worker in wood, a saddle-tree maker.
A Woodward was appointed to look after the King's interests in private woods within the forest.
Under forester and forester were officers of the crown employed to protect the 'vert and venison'.
Riders were employed to assist the agisters in the collection of marking fees.
A Ranger was required to look after the King's interest in the 'purlieus' - those areas once forest but later disafforested.
A Reeve was a representative of the manor or village concerned with its day to day running.

A Yeoman was a freehold farmer slightly higher in status than a Husbandman.

It should be remembered that many had dual occupations whilst others may have had more than one in their lifetimes. Men are rarely described as labourers in the New Forest before 1700 although they are in other parts of the county. Four people: John Pearce, Thomas Woolfe, Richard Osman and John Paynter are described thus in 1635 [DJS Cal 620, 626, 628/9] although all are described elsewhere as husbandmen. Four men were described as servants meaning labourers in 1677: Richard Osmond, Emanuell Osmond, [blank] Somers, and Michaell Whithorn. In the Hampshire wills and inventories index, which starts in 1570, it is not until 1746 that the first Minstead man is described as a labourer. Although there is another a year later, it is a further forty years before the third is shown.   Clearly some must have acted in this capacity, but only as a part of their livelihood. This would seem to reflect the forest way of life, where commoning was something that everyone did, allowing a certain sense of independence.

Appendix IV
London Minstead holdings in 1670 and their descent

These notes should be read in conjunction with the map on page 39 (figure 9). This is a composite map made up from a number of sources. No map of the area has been found earlier than 1787. The shapes of land have been taken from later known field boundaries. Whilst holdings have been worked out as carefully as possible there has, inevitably, been some use of 'best guess' given the available information in selection of fields within individual holdings.

The names used on the map are those which have had most general use in the records for holdings, they are not normally field names. The difficulty of tracing these items through rates lists is that the same family names occur frequently through the centuries.

A Manuscript map of 1787 and survey made by Abraham and William Driver together with one made in 1819 in connection with all the Lyndhurst Manor holdings provide a firm basis to locate properties.

Further connections can then be ascertained through lists of fuel rights which have been made at irregular intervals from 1670 to 1883. Many of the earlier ones were made at Lord Glenbervie's bidding around 1808, when a drive to reduce the number of properties with these rights was instigated.

1 Hobbs
This property is probably linked to Whitehorns in 1670. Deeds for Eugenie Cottage relate that Joseph Cabet purchased the property from Robert Hobbs prior to 1743. Cabet paid rates for three pieces of land called Whitehorns, How and his own. Widow Osmands comments, (Chapter 7) as a neighbour of Robert Over, may have been made from here, Whitehorns, or a cottage immediately to the south-west of Seamans. A William Osmond is shown as holding a cottage and plot of 1r 20p in 1655.

2 Whitehorns
The shape of the break between Hobbs and Whitehorns is seen on the earliest deeds for the former. It would seem from this shape that they were once one holding. The 1655 survey shows Robert Whitehorn holding an area of 1a 3r 18p; the tithe figure of 1838 for this plot and its neighbour (Hobbs) is 2a 0r 3p. A widow Whitehorn is shown in the hearth tax list for 1670.

3 Seamans
The Lyndhurst Manor court rolls show that Robert Over jnr had granted to him this holding in 1666. A further entry for 1719 grants the property to Zachariah Over and his sons Robert and John. Green Close and lands with buildings towards Seamans Lane

appear to be additions made after 1670 when the size grew to 11 acres. A John Hollis was the occupier in 1787; in 1793 the Reverend Joseph Hollis took possession.[1,2] E P Buckley later, possibly in 1801 certainly by 1808, had possession.[3]

4 Cheaters
John Chater made a claim for his messuage and land in 1635. His son, John Carter (Chater) claimed for one messuage and 8 acres in 1670.[4] The property can be traced through fuel lists and appears consistently in rates and land holdings schedules in the 18th and 19th centuries. Its size has remained unchanged for well over three centuries. Although it is better known as Pragnells now, the name John Prangnel has only been noted in rates lists around 1718. Moses House held the land in the early 1690's and William Gain had it in 1698. During the 18th century the Kent family acquired it. It was split during the early part of the 19th century with Joseph Kent retaining the southernmost fields whilst William Gain had the larger one (tithe 452). This was due to the estate being left by John Kent in 1807 to sons Aaron and Moses.[5]

5 Strides
Until 1626 Robert Hill held 4 acres of meadow, 4 acres of pasture, 4 acres of land (orchard, garden and messuage) and two acres of underwoods.[1] Although this total is larger than the 11 acres that Robert Hitchcock claimed under the same Manor in 1670 it is clearly the same property.[4] An almost identical description of the lands is made in 1737 when it passes from John Purkas to Edmund Waldron. Similarly a statement of 1819 shows that the underwoods, mentioned in 1626, are likely to be the omission of 1670, then known as Coal Heath Ground. From 1626 it was to be held by Christopher and Mary Jupe. In 1725 John Eldridge was the occupier, John Purkas was the holder in 1737 immediately prior to Edmund Waldron. The Waldrons held the property until July 1805 when it was granted to E P Buckley by which time it was known as Strides. It was used by Buckley to effect an exchange with William Gain in 1826.

6 Oldings
Although this area may be linked to an entry in the 1655 survey of Minstead Manor showing lands of 5a 2r 31p held by William Olding, this is by no means certain. The lands may not even have been a part of that manor at the time. A description of Caldoms to the south in 1735 gives details of possession and describes it thus '... garden, backside and lands formerly in the occupation of one Robert Hobbes on the north part and formerly were in the ?manurante tenure or occupation of one William Olding and since one Thomas Browne but now of one Richard Cull.'[6]

7 Paynters
Forest documents recording encroachments link this property to Harmans Grove.[7] It is not clear who held it in 1670. By 1787 it was in two pieces, one held by William Mansbridge and the other by Thomas White.[2] In 1838 the part held by Mansbridge, who had Perrys Farm across the road, was in two and occupied by James Perry. The other field

and homestead was then owned and occupied by Thomas White. Numbered 428 on the tithe map and covering 2a 2r 30p it passed, probably by marriage, into the Golden family (John Golden's second marriage to Catherine White) before being sold by son Joseph around 1863 to Mr William Preston of Minstead Lodge. It passed with the lodge thereafter until the cottage was pulled down, in the 1930's.

8 Oldings
This was held by Thomas Browne of Hinton Admiral who left a bequest for the poor of this and several other villages, the details of which are recorded in the Church.[18] His widow Joyce held the land in 1670 when it was shown to be 4 acres. Subsequently William Olding his nephew and 'legal heir' had the property alongside his other freehold and copyhold estates. It was held in the 1690's by Robert Tucker and then George Tucker until the 1720's. They left their mark in the field names of 'Tuckers Home Field' and 'Inner Tuckers'. John Kent was probably the next holder, he is confirmed in possession by 1743. It stayed with the Kents until, at least the 1850's when Jane Kent, widow of Joseph was in possession.[8] It was surrendered shortly after, in order that William Preston could effect an exchange with the Crown for lands he held at Lyndhurst during August 1864 to bring it into the Minstead Lodge estate.[9]

9 Caldoms
This was occupied by William Olding after Thomas Browne and then briefly by Robert Soffe, Robert Longman and Richard Cull before coming into the possession of the Kent family in or after 1735. The identically named heir of William Olding, who was a shipwright at Rumbridge, leased this four acre close to John Kent for 5s for 1 year.[6] It remained with the Kents until the 19th century when it was conveyed to Henry Combe Compton.

The name Caldoms doesn't appear in any of its forms (Caldams, Caldemes, Caldems, Caldomes, Caldoms, Caldrames, Caldrens, Caldumes, Caldums, Caldurnes, Calldoms) until the 1690's list. It may be based upon Caull's demesne land, Olding and John Caull were neighbours in the mid 17th century. Caull was evidently the chief or home farm tenant of Minstead Manor.

10 Harmans Grove
The early history of this holding is in chapter 7. John Kent leased the property from the Norris family in 1720 before purchasing it in 1750. It was possessed by him and his heirs until the middle of the 19th century when it became a part of the Minstead Lodge estate. Part of the holding was leased separately by 1782, initially to George Biggs and then Charles Bowles before being taken by E P Buckley and integrated into his estate.[10,5]

11 Rangers

Edward Ranger claimed forest rights for two messuages and six acres of land in Minstead and London Minstead in 1670. This is a tricky property to define. A field on the east side of the present Bull Lane if added to farm buildings and Howell's and Hay Rick fields comprises five and a half acres. The odd field, called Bulls, is shown on the 1819 map as belonging to Lyndhurst Manor and described as part of Kippernels whereas in 1787 it is freehold in the possession of John Mansbridge.[2] However the phrase 'copyhold part of Rangers Land' appears in a will of a neighbour made in 1681.[11]

The freehold of the property is much simpler. Francis Ranger had the land in the 1640's and 50's, after his death it was held by his widow prior to Edward Ranger's 1670 claim. A Charles Froud occupied it around 1720 before it became one of John Kent's acquisitions. It remained with the Kents until Joseph sold it in 1847 to Henry Compton for £500.[12]

12 Gains

The Gain family held this block of land from at least 1670 until 1826 when an exchange was made with E P Buckley to facilitate the latter's development of Minstead Lodge and consolidation of the grounds. The area in 1670 was 11 acres and remained the same into the 19th century. The land was enfranchised by Buckley's son, the Salisbury M.P., in 1846. The fuel rights had been extinguished 12 years earlier along with those of Little Keepings and Kippernels.[1,17]

13 Little Keepings

Amongst a draft list of particulars of grants in the New Forest in the early part of the 17th century is included 'One cott and two litle closes of pasture lyinge by ?pluc?ley lane in the occupa: of Jo: Paynter 1[ac] 1rd 18[pch]' Paynter, who died in 1626, held a customary tenancy of Lyndhurst Manor called Kippins which contained a messuage and land of around an acre.[1,13] Mentioned in a document of 1615 he is described as 'of London Mynsteed, in the countie of Southampton, husbandman, aged Lviij yeeres or thereaboutes'.[14] The property may well be linked to John Kippin of Minstead who left a will and inventory in 1612.[15]

By 1670 James Purcas had the holding which then included 2 acres. Held by Mary wife of John Scorey in 1752,[16] it remained with the Scoreys until 1778 when George Biggs of Romsey took the property. Eight years later the premises were surrendered by Biggs and taken up by Charles Bowles of Lymington, father of the poet Caroline. In 1787 the premises are described as a good brick house and land of 1a 2r 24p.[2] In March 1798 the premises passed from Captain Bowles to E P Buckley. Although the area was slightly less at 1a 2r 3p it was described as containing 'parts of Mansion house and park'.[1] Called Minstead Lodge in a list of fuel claims in 1809, it was enfranchised by Buckley's son in 1846.[3,1]

14 Kippernels

John Purcas occupied a cottage and two acres of land in 1670, the same premises were held by Mathew Purcas son of William in 1727 when there was 10 acres attached to it.[1] In the 1760's though still held by the Purcas family it consisted of 3 acres. By 1788 it included Bulls Field (tithe 422) in a total of 3a 3r 20p in John Mansbridge possession. Mansbridge retained it until after 1809 though by 1819 William Gain held it. He exchanged it with E P Buckley whose son enfranchised it in 1846.[1]

Notes and references

1   HRO 5M53/739 Court Rolls of Wriothesley Manors 1626-31; HRO 17M53 Court Roll of Lyndhurst manor; HRO 11M54; PRO F 10/60 Extracts from the Court Book of the Manor of Lyndhurst, Lyndhurst Copyholds 1819-1864

2   PRO F 17/250 Castle Malwood 10 ch to 1" map 1787; PRO F 20/48 Survey of the New Forest, 1787

3   PRO F 20/53 Appendices to Report to the Treasury, by Lord Glenbervie, on claims to fuel wood in the New Forest; with tables of names between 1670 and 1809, 1809

4   Abstract of Claims 1670, 1853 op. cit.

5   HRO 1801A49 John Kent will

6   HRO 70M87/7-12 Conveyance of Caldoms

7   D J Stagg, 1983 op. cit., 626

8   PRO PRO F 10/60 Lyndhurst Court Books 1819-64; Jane Kent was admitted to the premises, for her widowhood only, in October 1851

9   43rd Report of Her Majesty's Woods, Forests and Land Revenues, June 1865, Appendix 4; CRES 38 727 Lyndhurst lands near Pondhead, tithe nos. 276, 277, 278, 279. A Jane Kent, born in Minstead, was still living, aged 65, at Croydon in 1881

10 HRO 13M64/32-49 (BRA 1297) Deeds of Harmans Grove

11 HRO 1681A131 John Purkis will

12 HRO 70M87/13 Conveyance of Rangers

13 PRO E/147/6/11 Early 17th century New Forest particulars of grants

14 PRO E178/3097m.32&33 p. 4 Depositions concerning John Norden's sale and the use of a counterfeit axe in the New Forest dated 11 April, 1615

15 HRO 1612BO52/1-2 John Kippin will and inventory

16 HRO 149M89/R4/6137 Bedford papers: Fuel list of Lyndhurst Manor 1670 and 1752

17 11th Report of His Majesty's Woods, Forests and Land Revenues, July 1834, Appendix 8

18 Further details of his will are recorded in *Notes on the Parish Church, Lymington* by Charles Bostock and Edward Hapgood, Lymington, 1912, pp. 81-3

Appendix V
Coppice workers in 1575 at Hazel Hill, L Minstead

Amongst annual returns sent into the exchequer by the preservators in 1575 there is a list which appears to show the 'selling' of a part of the Forest. It is in fact the right to the underwoods that has been sold and provides an interesting example of forest coppice practice. Many of the names are familiar with the majority coming from Minstead, Bartley and Bramshaw.

Source: PRO E 101/142/15   Preservitors Returns, m.3

John Percher	1 acre	£4
Thomas Dowce gen	1 acre	£4 6s 8d
Thomas Lovell gen	1 acre	£4 6s 8d
Harry Stride	1½ acres & one yard	£6
Richard Lawrence	1 acre	£4 16s 8d
Symond Gauntlete	2 acres	£7 8s
William Hussey	2 acres	£7 8s
John Edmondes	1 acre	£4
John Clarke	1 acre	£4
Clement Androwes	1 acre	£4
John Croke	1 acre	£4
Richard Gosse	1 acre	£4 6s 8d
William Stryde	1 acre	£3 13s 4d
William Solfe	1 acre	£3 3s 4d
William Hobbes	5 acres	£12 13s 4d
Robert Buckett	1 acre	£1
William Warwicke	1 yard	13s 4d
Thomas Frynd	1 acre	£4 6s 8d
William Bowyer gen	1 acre	£4 13s 4d
Richard Hewett	1 acre	£4
John Sharpwell	1 acre	£4
Lord of Laytetter	1 acre	£4
Richard Marden	1 acre	£4
John Emlyn	1 acre	£3 13s 4d
John Hacker	1 acre	£2 13s 4d
John Colle	1 acre	£1 13s 4d
Richard Goosse	1 acre	£4
John Howker	1 acre	£1 13s 4d
William Stryde	1 acre	£2
Richard Tarvor	1 acre	£1 4s
William White	1½ acres	£3 6s 8d

William Warwicke	½ acre	£1
Rowland Horssey gen	1 acre	£4
John Henbest	1 acre	10s
John Purcas	1 little plot of wood	5s 4d
Richard Spenser	2 little parcells of wood	12s
36 people	40½ acres	£131 7s 4d

'the loppinges aforesaid as also this selling of the hill called clayhill and the hill called hassell hill we find to be an utter destrucon of the quenes tymber & wood'. 'Also we presente that the morefalls & boughes are marked with our ax but the kepers do take away the same and that Jo Stockeman hath rec all the somes of mony aforesaid & the ij hills not copsed.'

Notes
John Stockman apart from being keeper of Burley Bailiwick was the woodward. The largest block, 5 acres, was taken by William Hobbes whose property, Harmans Grove, was probably the closest. (See Chapter 7).

Appendix VI
Mini Biographies

Henry Bromfield, ca. 1610-1683. 1st son of Arthur and Lucy (née Quinby) JP. Originally of Chawcroft House, South Stoneham, Heywood House and manor at Boldre came into his possession through marriage to Frances Kemp. Held office in Lymington, being a free burgess in 1653 and Mayor in 1671. Elected to one of the two Lymington seats in parliament in 1660, he stood down a year later. Bowbearer in the forest 1662-69 he was also a verderer, possibly from 1670 until 1680. [*The Visitation of Hampshire and the Isle of Wight, 1686*, Ed G D Squibb, The Harleian Society, New Series,Vol 10 1991 p. 10; DJS 1670, 1494, Appendix B; *House of Commons 1660-1690* p. 724]

Thomas Browne, died 1667. Although described as of Hinton Admiral at his death, he was living in Minstead by 1649 and throughout the 1650's. His widow, Joyce, still held land in Minstead in 1670 as a tenant of Lyndhurst Manor. Profits from land he held near Christchurch were to be used for clothing and feeding the poor in eight local parishes. Details are in Bostock & Hapgood, *The Church in Lymington*, 1912, pp 81-3. The Minstead bequest is shown in the Church for distribution of bread on New Years Day together with a requirement that a certain sermon should be preached on the same day. He was a ranger of the Forest by the 1630's and continued so after the restoration until 1661. [HRO 53M80/PZ3 Sopley book of 19th and 20th century, p. 5; *Abstract of Claims 1670*, p 280, 278]

Phillip Dore, of Old Lymington, Mayor of Lymington 1652/3 [Old times revisited p. 183]. Along with John Hildesley and others was a trustee of Thomas Browne's will above. Held 5 messuages and 60 acres in London Minstead in 1670. Appeared at first court of Richard Compton at Minstead in 1652 but not thereafter . [*Abstract of Claims 1670*, p. 58 no. 62, DJS 1669 1430, *Hearth Tax 1665*, 161]

Richard Goddard, ca. 1590-1666. Son of Richard of Southampton and Elizabeth née Dauntsey. Married firstly in 1615, Mary daughter of Edward Nicholls of All Cannings, Wilts and lived at nearby Etchilhampton. Second marriage was to the widow of John Nevey of Southampton. He was elected MP for Winchester in 1661 which he held until his death. He had a sizable house (ten hearths) in Bartley Regis in 1665. He appears in Minstead court minutes as a freeholder in 1652, selling his land to Richard Belbyn prior to October 1656. In 1654 he is referred to as 'the late Steward of the said [Minstead] Mannor'. He is also stated to have been Steward to the Forest prior to the Civil War as well as from 1660-5. He was taken prisoner by the Roundheads and after his release settled in Salisbury. He is recorded as a Verderer by 1632 and until at least 1635. The same year he claimed forest rights for 100 acres and a messuage at Bartley Regis. No connection is known between this Goddard and the family of the same name at Birchenwood, Bramshaw. [*House of Commons 1660-1690* p. 402; Rev A W Stote mss Soc of Genealogists, Ac. 29232; *Hearth Tax 1665*, 95; PRO C99 41 no. 233]

Jonathan Godfrey, an active land surveyor from around 1630 to 1658, was a partner to Joseph Blagrave of Berkshire. They called themselves 'practical mathematicians' in 1630, a term often used for surveyors. Godfrey termed himself 'artist' so possibly specialised in the making and decoration of maps. His best known local work is the 1657 map of Portswood. He worked in Oxfordshire, Berkshire and Hampshire. [*Dictionary of Land Surveyors,* 1997, Sarah Bendall; *The Local Historian*, Nov 1993, Vol 23 No 4 Some eighteenth-century chain surveyors, Patricia Preece pp. 218-227]

John Hildesley, ca. 1598-1681 of Hinton Admiral. A Free burgess of the Borough of Lymington 1635, though a non resident, he was also mayor of Christchurch on three occasions in the 1630's. As a strong supporter of parliament he was an elected member for Hampshire, Winchester and Christchurch through the 1650's until the restoration in 1660. He worked as a JP, permission being required from him for timber in the forest for church repairs in Minstead in 1646. A note made in the Forest Eyre of 1670 indicates that he held a number of forest records, either from his time as a Justice or as Sheriff in 1656/7. [*House of Commons 1660-90* Vol 2 pp. 548-9; Edward King, *Old Times Revisited in the borough and parish of Lymington*, 1879, 1976 reprint, Barry Shurlock, Winchester, p. 188; DJS 1670 1471]

William Olding ca. 1630-1700. A farmer, timber merchant, carrier of the king's timber and property developer of Minstead. First recorded in Minstead in 1652 he was described as a kinsman of Robert Olding of Eling (Pottersford) in 1662. He held 11 acres of copyhold land from Minstead Manor in 1652 and added to this seven acres of freehold from Roger Collins in 1655. A further 3 acres called Trumps he farmed by 1656 in addition to four acres of Caldoms. By 1670 he was holding 25 acres of land, he later acquired a further 4 acres of Lyndhurst Manor land at London Minstead formerly leased by Thomas Browne and his widow Joyce. Olding's wife, Susannah, is believed to have been a sister to Thomas Browne. He may have moved to Ellingham towards the close of the century but retained the freehold land in the village. The burial of a widow, Joan Olding, wife of William, buried at Ellingham in 1708, may indicate a second marriage or be his daughter-in-law. He was on the parish vestry committee from 1653, played an active part as tythingman in the capture of armed felons, and a conscientious churchwarden. In the Forest he was a regarder in the 1660's and acted as a witness against the Crown in a case of timber seizure in 1670 at Bramshaw despite being a carrier of the king's timber. [HRO 1662AO71/1-2 Inventory Robert Olding; *Cal of St Pap Dom 1670* p 97; 1677 Inquiry PRO E 178 6453 Commission of Inquiry; 1729A101 Will of William Olding (son?) of Ellingham; DJS Appendix B]

Francis Sambrooke, Salisbury based, may have been the son of Francis Sambrooke a Salisbury Tailor. Steward of Richard Compton's Hampshire Manors from 1652 he may have obtained the position through connection with Richard Goddard above mentioned. He was Deputy clerk of the peace at Salisbury by 1662 and still in post in 1666. [WRS 15, item 497 1620; WRS 11, p. ix, p. xlv; WRS 43 item 32]

Edward Willougby died 1623. He is recorded in 1604 as a regarder of the Forest and in 1609 a ranger, a post he retained until at least 1622. He lived at London Minstead in a simple messuage with twelve acres of land. Although not well off he was described as a Gentleman in official reports. His inventory confirms this and indicates that he wore a mark of his appointment as Ranger. [PRO E/101/143/1. m. 3 & 4; PRO E/147/6/11 Early 17th century New Forest particulars of grants; DJS Appendix B]

Sources

DJS (year) followed by numbers refers to D J Stagg, *A Calendar of New Forest Documents 15th to 17th centuries*, Hampshire Record Series Vol V, 1983, Winchester
Abstract of Claims 1670 HMSO 1853
Hearth Tax *The Hampshire Hearth Tax Assessment 1665*, Ed Elizabeth Hughes and Philippa White, Hampshire Record Series Vol XI, 1991, Winchester
House of Commons 1660-1690 B D Henning, *History of Parliament, The House of Commons 1660-90*, 1983
WRS Wiltshire Record Society, Devizes

Glossary

Affeerer Person chosen to assess penalties in a manorial court.

Amercement A non-fixed penalty in a manorial court.

Assart Land converted from forest into arable use illegally.

Bailiwick One of nine Forest administration areas.

Chaffing dish A vessel to hold burning charcoal and used for cooking. [OED]

Colefire So much firewood as (when it is burnt) contains a load of coals. [E Coles An English Dictionary, 1676, Georg Olms Reprint 1973]

Expediting Maiming a dog so that it would not pull down a deer.

Forest An area over which forest law applied.

Forest Law Code built up to protect the kings favoured hunting grounds.

Fusterer A saddle tree maker, the wooden support for pack saddles.

Groomkeeper The forest keeper on the ground who looked after the 'vert and venison'. Also known as an underforester or underkeeper, there were sometimes two or three to a Bailiwick.

Heriot A due payable to the Lord of a manor on the death of a tenant - usually the best beast.

Homage Jury.

Husbandman A copy or lease hold tenant farmer often little different from a labourer.

Imbowes Branches of trees in which honey was found.

King's Woodward His duty was to assign, fell and sell timber.

Load 2 to 2½ cords of wood made a load of charcoal. A cord of wood weighed about 2 loads. A load of charcoal may have been a horseload of 12 sacks each of 1 cwt. See G. Hammersley, 1957, op. cit. p 156.

Lugg   Area of land, 5$^1/_2$ yds square.

Master Keeper   An appointment held under the Lord Warden to look after a Bailiwick - in practice a sinecure - see Groomkeeper.

Messuage   Dwelling and land assigned to its use.

Pillory   Punishment post for head and arms to be tied to or go through.

Preservator   Forest officer required to report on the timber to the Exchequer.

Purlieu   An area previously forest to which some forest laws still applied.

Purpresture   An encroachment.

Ranger   Forest officer who was required to look after the purlieus.

Regarder   Forest Officer required to answer chapters (questions) of the regard before a forest court.

Reeve   Representative of a town or 'vill'.

Relief   A payment to the lord of the manor on property changing hands.

Tumbrel   Cucking or ducking stool.

Underforester   See Groomkeeper.

Underkeeper   See Groomkeeper.

Underwoods   Trees and saplings other than timber trees growing in a wood.

Vert   The forest in which the object of the hunt lived.

Vicinage   Customary intercommoning without additional payment or right.

Walk   Area looked after by a Groomkeeper, at one time synonymous with Bailiwick but later a subdivision of this.

Woodward   An officer who protected the deer and their habitat in private woodlands within a forest.

Yeoman   A freehold farmer.

Select Bibliography

Forest Law

Boulton, Helen E., [Ed.] *The Sherwood Forest Book*, Thoroton Society Record Series Vol XXIII, 1965.

Fisher, W.R., *The Forest of Essex*, Butterworths, 1887.

fitz Nigel, Richard, Dialogue of the Exchequer, in *English Historical Documents 1042-1189*, pp 490-569, Eyre and Spottiswoode, 1953.

Grant, Raymond., *The Royal Forests of England, Alan Sutton, Stroud, 1991.

Hart, C., *The Verderers and Forest Laws of Dean*, David & Charles, Newton Abbot, 1971.

Manwood, J., *A Treatise of the Lawes of the Forest*, 1615.

MacDermot, Edward T., *The History of the Forest of Exmoor*, 1911 (Rev Ed, David & Charles, Newton Abbot, 1973).

Nicholls, H.G., *The Forest of Dean; an Historical and Descriptive Account*, 1858 (reprint David & Charles, Dawlish, 1966).

Petit-Dutaillis, C., *Studies and Notes supplementary to Stubbs' Constitutional History*, Vol 2, Manchester Univ. Press, Manchester, 1915.

Pettit, P.A.J., *The Royal Forests of Northamptonshire 1558-1714*, Northants Record Society, 1968.

New Forest and Hampshire

Aitchison, Selina,*The Ancient Manors of Minstead and Bisterne,* Winchester, 1906.

Chapman, J. & Seeliger, S., *Formal and Informal Enclosures in Hampshire 1700-1900,* Hampshire Papers, 1997.

Chapman, J. & Seeliger, S., *A Guide to Enclosure in Hampshire,* Hampshire County Council, Hampshire Record Series Vol XV, Winchester, 1997.

Coleby, A.M., *Central Government and the Localities Hampshire 1649-1689,* CUP, Cambridge, 1987.

Fearon, W.A. & Williams, J.F., *Hampshire Registers*, Wykeham Press, Winchester, 1909, introduction.

Doubleday, A., & Page, W. [Eds] *Victoria County History, Hampshire*, 5 Vols 1900-14.

Furley, J.S., *Quarter Sessions Government in Hampshire in the Seventeenth Century,* Wykeham Press, Winchester. ca. 1937.

Godwin, G.N., *The Civil War in South West Hampshire*, Southampton, 1886.

Hockey, Dom F., *Beaulieu King John's Abbey*, Pioneer Publications, Beaulieu, 1976.

Hughes, Elizabeth & White, Philippa, *The Hampshire Hearth Tax Assessment 1665*, [Eds] Elizabeth Hughes and Philippa White, Hampshire Record Series Vol XI, Winchester, 1991.

Kenchington, F.E., *The Commoners New Forest*, Hutchinson, 1944.

Marshall, William, *The Review and Abstract of the County Reports to the Board of Agriculture,* Volume 5: Southern and Peninsular, 1817 (reprint Augustus Kelley, New York, 1968).

McClelland, E.M. & Hall, P., *Woodgreen: Village without title*, ca. 1983/4.

Russell, Valerie, *New Forest Ponies*, David & Charles, Newton Abbot, 1976.

Stagg, D.J., *A Calendar of New Forest Documents 1244-1334*, Hampshire Record Series, Vol III, Winchester, 1979.

Stagg, D.J., *A Calendar of New Forest Documents 15th to 17th centuries*, Hampshire Record Series Vol V, Winchester, 1983.

Sumner, H. *The Earthworks of the New Forest*, Chiswick Press, 1917.

Tavener, L.E., *The Common Lands of Hampshire*, Hampshire County Coumcil, ca 1957.

Tubbs, C.R., *The New Forest An Ecological History*, David & Charles, Newton Abbott, 1968.

Tubbs, C.R., *The New Forest A Natural History*, Collins, 1986.

Farming

Barley, M.W., *The English Farmhouse and Cottage*, Routledge & Kegan Paul, 1961.

Bettey, J.H., *Rural Life in Wessex 1500-1900*, Gloucester, 1987.

Butlin, R.A., The enclosure of common fields and extinction of common rights in England, circa 1600-1750: a review by, in Fox, H.S.A. & Butlin, R.A., *Change in the Countryside*: Essays on Rural England 1500-1900, Institute of British Geographers, London, 1979.

Clay, C., [Ed] *Rural society: landowners, peasants and labourers 1500-1750,* Chapters from The Agrarian History of England and Wales Gen. Ed. Joan Thirsk, CUP, Cambridge, 1990.

Fussell, G.E., *The English Rural Labourer*, The Batchworth Press, 1949. (Part 1).

Fussell, G.E. & K.R., *The English Countryman*, 1955, (Bloomsbury Books reprint 1985).

Neeson, J.M., *Commoners: Common Right, Enclosure and Social Change in England, 1700-1820,* CUP, 1993.

Orwin, C.S., *A History of English Farming*, T Nelson, 1949.

Seebohm, M.E., *The Evolution of the English Farm*, 1927, (2nd ed reprinted 1976, Wakefield).

Stamp, L. Dudley, & Hoskins, W.G., *The Common Lands of England and Wales*, Collins, 1963.

Stratton, J.M., Houghton Brown, Jack, Ed Ralph Whitlock, *Agricultural Records A.D. 220-1977*, John Baker, 1978.

General

Braun, Hugh, *Elements of English Architecture,* David & Charles, Newton Abbott, 1973.

Crossley, D.W., *Sidney Ironworks Accounts 1541-1573*, Royal Historical Society, Camden 4th Series Vol 15, 1975.

Firth & Rait, *Acts and Ordinances of the Interregnum*, 3 vols, 1911.

Harvey, P.D.A., *Manorial Records British Records Association Archives and the User,* No 5 1984.

Hone, N.J., *The Manor and Manorial Records*, Methuen, 1906.

Hughes, Edward, *Studies in Administration and Finance 1558-1825*, Manchester, 1934.

Larkin James F. & Hughes, Pauk L., *Stuart Royal Proclamations*, Oxford, 1973 2 vols.

Madge, Sidney J, *The Domesday of Crown Lands*, Routledge, 1938.

March, Earl of (Charles Henry Gordon-Lennox) *Records of the Old Charlton Hunt*, Elkin Mathews, Vigo Street 1910.

Parry, R.H., [Ed] *The English Civil War and After 1642-1658,* Macmillan, London 1970.

Spufford, Margaret, The limitations of the probate inventory - pp 139-174. in Chartres, John & Hey, David, [Eds] *English Rural Society, 1500-1800, Essays in honour of Joan Thirsk,* CUP, 1990. [This highlights weaknesses, in particular the difference shown between inventories which do not show accounts and those where they are available throwing a different light on the wealth of individuals].

Vinogradoff, P. *The Growth of the Manor,* Allen & Unwin, 1904, 3rd Ed 1920.

Index

The text has been indexed throughout. The appendices, apart from the first, have been indexed for personal names only. Variations of a surname are shown in brackets, these have not been cross-referenced as the alternatives would generally appear close to the master entry. Where a village of a person, other than Minstead, is known, it appears in brackets. An attempt has been made to link items under subject headings.

Symbols

1692 Bill 22
1801 Commission 43

A

Acres Down 45, 109
Acts of Parliament
  ...Abrogate the Forest Law (1971) 11
  Against the erection and maintaining of cottages (1588-9) 28
  Inclosing of Woods in Forests (1482) 11
  Increase and Preservation of Timber in the New Forest (1698) 22, 79–80, 84, 85
  Poor Relief (1601) 101
  Poor Relief (1662) 102
  Preservation of Woods (1543) 11
  Relief of Soldiers and Mariners (1601) 103
  Timber not to be felled for making coals (1558) 79
Alder 45, 78
Alehouses 31, 63
Androwes, Clement 134
Animals. *See* Stock and Dogs
Ansell, Phillip 30, 91, 104–105, 108
Apprentices 102
Archer, Michael 109
Arundel, Mrs 6
Arundell, Lord 7
Ash 78
Ashdown Forest 5
Ashe, Giles (Fordingbridge) 102
Ashurst 107
Assault 91
Audly, Henry (Woodward) 16

B

Bacon, Cuthbert (Riding Forester) 19

S